DITCH THE WORTHINESS HUSTLE

Getting Real About Driven Woman Syndrome and Leading From Your Edge

Charlie McClain

Wild Femmepreneur

Las Vegas, Nevada

For permission requests, email assistant@leadfromyouredge.co
Lead From Your Edge | Wild Femmepreneur
leadfromyouredge.co
Ditch the Worthiness Hustle/Charlie Mac – 1st ed.
ISBN 9798890901743

— ♥ —

To my children, Nicholas and Anna,

and to Riff Raff.

Thank you for being in my soul cluster.

I love you.

CONTENTS

FORWARD

In the ever-evolving landscape of business and entrepreneurship, women have risen to the occasion, shattered glass ceilings, and carved out their unique path to success. In what is often a dynamic, high-pressured, and all-encompassing journey, one remarkable individual has emerged as a guiding light, a beacon of wisdom, and an unwavering source of inspiration for countless women in business. Her name is Charlie McClain, and her impact on the lives of leaders and entrepreneurs is nothing short of extraordinary.

This book is a testament to the transformative power of Charlie's coaching and mentorship. As you turn the pages, you will embark on a journey of personal and professional growth guided by the insights, strategies, and unwavering support of a coach who has dedicated her life to empowering women in business.

Charlie understands that the path to success is rarely linear. It is filled with twists, turns, and unexpected challenges. Yet, she knows that with the right guidance and mindset, every obstacle can become an opportunity, and every setback can fuel a comeback. Through her expertise, she equips women with the tools they need to not only survive but thrive in the business world.

This book is a treasure trove of wisdom and practical advice that Charlie has amassed over years of dedicated coaching. Her insights on leadership, the subconscious, emotion regulation, and resilience will empower you to unlock your full potential and confidently lead. Whether you're a seasoned leader, entrepreneur, or just beginning your journey, you'll find invaluable lessons and actionable strategies that can propel you to greater heights.

Beyond the methods and techniques, what truly sets Charlie apart is her unwavering belief in the potential of every woman she mentors. Her genuine care, encouragement, and commitment to her clients go far beyond the conventional coach-client relationship. She becomes a trusted friend, a cheerleader, and a source of unwavering support as you strive to master the art of having it all.

Throughout this book, you will encounter stories of women who have transformed their lives and businesses under Charlie's guidance. Their stories testify to her profound impact on those fortunate enough to work with her. They stand as living proof that you can overcome any obstacle and achieve greatness with this incredible coach at your side.

As you delve into the pages of this book, open your heart and mind to the possibilities that lie ahead. Know that you are not alone on this journey. Charlie McClain is with you every step of the way, offering her expertise, wisdom, and unwavering support.

She gives a fuck. She walks her walk, she cares deeply and genuinely about seeing other women succeed, and she is beyond generous with her content, her wisdom, and her energy. I should know. I have not only followed her work for years but have also been fortunate enough to have cultivated a friendship with her over time. I've witnessed her commitment to boldly and generously supporting other women leaders.

So, with great excitement and anticipation, I invite you to embark on this transformative journey with Charlie McClain. Let her be your guiding star, mentor, and source of inspiration as you navigate the exciting and challenging world that is quintessentially female leadership. Your success story begins here in the pages of this book and continues with the invaluable guidance of a truly exceptional executive and leadership coach.

Get ready to unlock your full potential, break through blocks, and achieve the success you've always dreamed of. The journey starts now, and it begins with this book.

Here's to your limitless potential and boundless success!

Trina Serrecchia, CPC | ELI MP | PCC | PMP

INTRODUCTION

You can make money in business without doing the deep inner work. I did. I went decades without doing it. I built a successful career and even developed side hustle companies along the way. A couple of them did pretty well–all without me even having to know myself. But this book isn't about money or success. This book is about being free to lead from your edge *without* the worthiness hustle. It's about getting on a path that will eventually lead to being unapologetically, unequivocally, unbridled *you*. So let me ask you: How well do you know you?

Trauma is a strange beast, seizing ahold of our neural pathways and taking up a permanent space in our brain's real estate. I'll get into why this is so important later, but for now, let me ask you: Do you know what kind of eggs you like?

As I write this, it has almost been twelve years since I was a homeless, bankrupt, abuse victim who had divorced for the second time in three years. The first marriage had been 13 years of primarily mental abuse.

I had to flee for my life from the second one. What I came to understand at 46 was that I had yet to really understand who I was. I was like the character Maggie Carpenter (played by Julia Roberts) in Runaway Bride. She didn't know what type of eggs she liked because whatever each man Maggie dated liked, she always went with that.

I had been doing the 'Worthiness Hustle.' You know, the pleasing, per-forming, perfecting habits that, for me, had set up a lifetime of choos-ing unhealthy relationships. And because those habits were so familiar,

I didn't recognize that I was emotionally drowning in Fight, Flight, Freeze, Flop, and Fawn.

And then, one day, I took a good, hard look in the mirror and heard my own voice in my mind. It said, "If you stay here, you will be dead soon." I recognized that truth deep in my bones. I had to get out of there and change my life.

Long story short. I did just that. It was terrifying and complicated, but I did it. What haunted me was that I still didn't know what kind of eggs I liked. You know?

As I took the tender, sometimes painful baby steps of my recovery, I discovered I needed to spend more time working on the most important relationship in my life: The one with myself. It had always been so much easier to focus on everything going on outside of me, and those relationships were something I could *do* something about. And *doing* is what I did best–allowing myself to come from *being* scared the shit out of me. Who would I find in that silence and solitude? Who would greet me at the door? Did *she* have any real value? I mean, *her* relationship choices clearly weren't the best. *Those men* hadn't valued her. *They* hadn't treated her very well. Therefore, Something must be wrong with *her*.

Of course, facing the question of my self-worth was precisely what I didn't want to do. But I knew that another of *those* relationships was much more likely if I didn't take the time to figure out what kind of eggs I liked. I needed to find myself and face all the truths that came with that journey. And that journey for each of us is what this book is about.

Along the way, I'll share snippets of my own experiences and those of my clients. I'll offer some clarity on Driven Woman Syndrome and share some practical steps to begin to ditch your own worthiness hustle so you can get on the path to lead from your edge.

— ONE —

The Worthiness Hustle
(Driven Woman Syndrome)

Pleasing. Performing. Perfecting. Every woman I've ever said those words to immediately nods her head. Never has a woman said, "What do you mean?" But I will tell you what I mean anyway.

We come into this world completely open, ready to learn the structure of our family—our tribe. Along the way, we come to understand the practicalities, such as the hot stove and not running into the street. And then, we are taught the rules of our tribe, starting with our immediate family and branching out.

If you think about it, the rules we must learn by age six or seven are remarkably complicated. Unfortunately, during these formative years, we learn some rules that either don't serve us or are, simply put, false representations of what is safe, good, bad, or achievable. And depending on who or what taught us these things, false core beliefs are certainly tucked away in our subconscious.

In a nutshell, layers and layers of programming have determined what we believe about our world and ourselves. Most of these layers are so hidden beneath others that even identifying some of them is the figurative needle in the haystack.

We are taught statements like the following:

Girls are sugar, spice, and everything nice.

Girls shouldn't play rough or make too much noise.

Silence is golden.

Never argue or question authority; girls (women) who do will suffer for it.

Don't act tough! But never be emotional at work.

If you are tough, you are a bitch.

If you are fair, you are soft.

Women can't be good leaders; they're too emotional.

Women can't be <u>fantastic career choice here.</u>

Actually, I couldn't say it better than Gloria from Barbie (2023):

> It is literally impossible to be a woman. You are so beautiful and so smart, and it kills me that you don't think you're good enough. Like, we have to always be extraordinary, but somehow we're always doing it wrong.
>
> You have to be thin but not too thin. And you can never say you want to be thin. You have to say you want to be healthy, but also you have to be thin. You have to have money, but you can't ask for money because that's crass. You have to be a boss, but you can't be mean. You have to lead, but you can't squash other people's ideas. You're supposed to love being a mother but don't talk about your kids all the damn time. You have to be a career woman but also always be looking out for other people.
>
> You have to answer for men's bad behavior, which is insane, but if you point that out, you're accused of complaining. You're supposed to stay pretty for men but not so pretty that you tempt them too much or that you threaten other women because you're supposed to be a part of the sisterhood.

But always stand out and always be grateful. But never forget that the system is rigged. So find a way to acknowledge that but also always be grateful.

You have to never get old, never be rude, never show off, never be selfish, never fall down, never fail, never show fear, never get out of line. It's too hard! It's too contradictory, and nobody gives you a medal or says thank you! And it turns out, in fact, that not only are you doing everything wrong, but also everything is your fault.

I'm just so tired of watching myself and every single other woman tie herself into knots so that people will like us. And if all of that is also true for a doll just representing women, then I don't even know.

Yep. Layers of programming. And that's just from our larger culturescape. A myriad of events and circumstances add layers of imprints and false beliefs. What results is a lot of pleasing, performing, and perfecting behaviors that rule our choices and then our circumstances.

I want to take this opportunity to say that we pile on additional layers from childhood experiences and childhood trauma. I must point out that Childhood PTSD is real. And there are literally no rules about which experiences *qualify* as trauma. In working with my clients, I see this hidden rule all of the time.

It goes, "But is what I went through tragic or devastating enough to *count* as trauma?" My answer is always the same: What did it feel like for you? *That* is what counts.

Since children often cannot understand that their body's response is a reaction to chronic trauma, their behavior patterns follow them into adulthood, even when their environment is seemingly safe. As a result of responding to constant trauma, their stress response is hyperactive. It causes an increase in adrenaline and cortisol at the slightest perceived threat.

This doesn't necessarily mean we are always hyper-responding to *everything*. What it explains is our hyper-response to *some* things.

The good news is that we don't need to relive the programming to recognize and learn to transcend it.

Awareness is truly half the battle. Let me tell you about Cassandra:

Cassy is my client and former high-level executive of a Fortune 500 company gone rogue. In other words, Cassy wanted to start a new season where *her* dreams were at the center of her workload rather than that of, as she so aptly put it, "...a corporation that treated her more like a cog than a human."

A friend had contacted me and mentioned Cassy's struggle to find her confidence again now that she was the CEO of her own foundation. According to our mutual friend, she was experiencing feeling a bit like an 'imposter.' This may seem surprising since we know Cassy came from a high-intensity, very male-driven environment where confidence is 'king.' She was a corporate badass! Why on earth would she feel like an imposter?

Statistically, a vast percentage of high performers feel this way. In fact, among driven women, this is entirely the norm. And this is what I explained to Cassy in our 90-minute courtesy conversation.

Cassy and I met for the first time via Zoom. This was pre-pandemic, but we were both veterans of virtual meetings due to our corporate day jobs. A bit nervous, though, Cassy explained her dissatisfaction that plagued her life before she decided to start her foundation; these feelings still made her shrink into herself as she described them.

"Let me ask you," I responded, "You seem almost as though you want to hide from feeling dissatisfied, even now. Why is that?"

Immediately, the tears welled in her eyes. "Because I have a perfect life," she almost yelled, "I don't have the right to feel dissatisfied!"

And yet, that is precisely how Cassy had felt. Earning high six figures, having two kids, and a loving partner was the life she had envisioned and created for herself. Cassy had worked two jobs to get through college, suffering many sleepless nights, and spent decades working her way up the proverbial corporate ladder. But she was almost ashamed of her success because it still wasn't enough.

Cassy wanted more. She had climbed the mountain she felt she was supposed to want to climb, only to find there was a whole other journey she wanted to take.

Upon reflection, Cassy didn't regret that mountain; she just wanted a different expedition planned by herself rather than by family, society, or a corporation. And this made her feel incredibly selfish and unworthy. Anyone who knew Cassy envied her. She seemed to have it all. How dare she require more?

But the idea of starting a foundation kept tugging at her. Late at night, when she knew she *should be* running the latest quarterly metrics through her mind as usual, she instead fantasized about helping families struggling to raise a child with a disability. Cassy had a sister who was a single mom of a son with muscular dystrophy. The father hadn't been able to cope, knowing his son wasn't likely to experience his 30s, but Dad did pay child support. However, Cassy's sister just didn't have the resources she needed. And even after reluctantly accepting Cassy's help, her sister had suffered relentlessly.

Her nephew had died the previous year at age 22. Cassy knew that a foundation like the one she envisioned could make a difference in real people's lives. She imagined her sister being on the board.

Here is the point of my telling you this story: Cassy had all the things she was told she should want from life. She even made her dream come true and did start that foundation. Her sister is indeed on the board. But when Cassy came to me, she felt just like the rest of us mere mortals. She felt shame and guilt for having dreams beyond her responsibilities. And she felt undeserving and afraid. When she achieved the goals she set, instead of feeling proud of herself, she felt like someone was going to come along any moment, point a finger, and say, "Get that fraud out of here!"

While this story doesn't get into Cassy's history, trust me when I tell you there's a lifetime of impossible standards, high expectations, and habits of pleasing, performing, and perfecting that Cassy has uncovered and dealt with as we continued to work together. Cassy has Driven Woman Syndrome.

Driven Woman Syndrome is self-diagnosed, has no cure, and can't be improved with a pill.

I first used the term "Driven Woman Syndrome" in my Master's Thesis, written mainly in 2019-2020. I won't claim I was the first to coin it, but after countless hours of research, I haven't found the person who did.

Based on my extensive research then, Driven Woman Syndrome refers to a phenomenon where highly motivated and successful women become so dedicated to their careers and personal goals (including goals of pleasing others) that they neglect their well-being and relationships. This leads to the very real experience of burnout, stress, and unhappiness.

I use the term 'very real' because so many women are gaslit regarding the associated effects, conditions, and experiences of burnout and stress; it's important to me to mention that these experiences are not imagined or exaggerated.

Studies have shown that women are more likely than men to experience work-family conflict, which can lead to prolonged feelings of guilt and stress.

The pressure to "have it all" can also contribute to the development of Driven Woman Syndrome. Our culturescape often sends the message that women should be successful in their careers, have a happy family life, and maintain a pristine appearance, all while balancing a demanding workload and social life. Even without challenging family relationships or trauma, this societal programming can lead women to believe that they must constantly strive for more, even at the expense of their own happiness and well-being.

The symptoms of Driven Woman Syndrome can include exhaustion, anxiety, depression, and a general feeling of being overwhelmed. Women who suffer from this syndrome may struggle with finding a healthy work-life balance and may also experience challenges within their personal relationships.

At this point, you may be exclaiming, "That's me!" Or, you may be thinking that based on my definition, all women probably have Driven Woman Syndrome.

To these considerations, I say yes. It is also me. And yes, the number of women I know who'd qualify as having Driven Woman Syndrome is shocking. But that doesn't make the definition any less accurate. Nor is it surprising if you think about it. The experience of today's woman is just as real as the experience of today's man. We've evolved. And there are consequences for it. Many of us are stressed, anxious, and just plain exhausted from jumping through hoops, regardless of who created them. At the same time, there doesn't often seem to be viable options to replace those hoops.

Recognizing ourselves as having a genuine experience that needs our attention isn't about blame. Instead, it is about our own well-being and ability to foster future generations of healthy, successful women who lead balanced and fulfilling lives.

Moving forward, our conversation is about more than resilience; it is about mastering ourselves, prioritizing self-care, and setting boundaries in our personal and professional lives. It is about taking time for ourselves, delegating tasks, and learning to say "no" when necessary. It's about regulating our thoughts, our nervous system, and our mind. In the beginning, it's about standing in front of the mirror.

I'll go first: As a professional with a day job, I can tell you that it has been a constant struggle for me to feel 'satisfied' with my career and myself. It's sort of always been that way.

Initially, I felt dissatisfied because I grew up poor. Later, it was my lack of a healthy relationship. And so I poured my efforts into changing those two things. Later, when I lived in a million-dollar home and was out-earning my husband, I was dissatisfied for the same reasons. However, my situation was somewhat unique. My husband was a narcissist who controlled my money and the minutia of my life, right down to my clothing– except–when I was at work.

His financial abuse had been horrible. Here I was, married to a millionaire, and the only way I could purchase the items I needed for myself and my two children was to 'sneak' purchase them via a secret credit card. To be perfectly honest, the experience of freedom to make my own choices was thrilling, and I continued to accrue debt for items that I didn't need at all.

Being 'caught' for my 15k of debt led to years of cyclic behavior and serious verbal and occasional physical abuse. Worse, my children were caught up in it. My son had been diagnosed with ADHD, and my husband's solution was a 'corporal' method of punishment that involved countless hours of the push-up position and constant grounding.

For many years, my daughter was the 'good' child, staying out of trouble and in his good graces. She was his supply. Until she wasn't.

After I had sent my son to live with his father, my daughter became my husband's only focus, particularly since I was always working. Initially, this seemed promising, as she earned his praises and trust. But the year she started middle school, she began to have challenges with grades and dramatic relationships with her friends.

As a woman, I'm sure you know exactly what I mean. This happens. But for my husband, this was a betrayal. She no longer lived up to his expectations or his vision of her. My daughter's fallible teenage experience proved to him she was too much like me. This meant she could also end up a "liar, cheater, and thief," which is what he called me since my escapades with personal credit. Many years later, I understood this was about control, of course, and my daughter becoming a teen had challenged his power, just as my debt had.

He verbally abused me. And now, he verbally abused her. You bet I left. But it still makes me wince to write that it took me four more years and countless hours of therapy to do it. Unfortunately, I left with almost nothing due to a prenup and my lack of energy to fight him. After 13 years together, my now 16-year-old daughter and I left with only our clothes, a box of dishes, and roughly 30,000.

Let me tell you why I am sharing this story with you, because it does get worse, to a genuinely embarrassing level:

The onion layers of programming can land the most amazing women into the strangest of circumstances.

Within 18 months, I was married again to a physically abusive con artist. And that marriage cost me my relationship with my daughter for almost two years, all of my retirement money, and what was left of my self-esteem. I had given him my money and my mojo to start a business for him.

And as I built and ran that business for him, the truth began to reveal itself. He wasn't who he claimed to be; was hundreds of thousands of dollars in debt, and *that* was why the business had to be in my name–and much, too much more to mention here.

The police came to my door twice, and I did the thing I had previously only seen on TV. I sent them away. Does *this* woman sound like a successful boss babe to you? She didn't to me either.

Just a few months before that, some friends had staged an intervention. I cried and got mad at *them*. But the words of those fantastic women stayed with me. They thought I was worth something. They saw more in me than I did. They believed in me and in my ability to build a good life for myself.

Eighteen months later, I fled that marriage for my life, having signed the business over to a partner. Now homeless, I spent some time at a battered woman's shelter, completely isolated myself from anyone who knew me, and legally changed my name so he couldn't find me.

I did have my son, but that came with some challenges. He had recently come back into my life. And while our journey together is truly a book of its own, I will briefly explain that his ADHD had now become something much more challenging. And so I took him with me to Washington, where my Auntie lived. Being estranged from my father since I was six, Auntie had only been back in my life for about ten years.

This wonderful, trusting woman gave us a place to stay for a few weeks. But I have always been a driven woman. So, in just 14 days, I had gotten a new job in Austin, Texas, and packed the car.

January 2013 was the beginning of my new life. I was 47.

When I looked in the mirror, what I found was myself, hidden underneath many layers of programming. So when I tell you that the worthiness hustle can cost more than business success or make a mess of our personal relationships—and when I tell you that it is possible to ditch that worthiness hustle and build whatever life you wish for yourself, I speak from experience.

So let's do this!

— TWO —

Digging Ditches

Let me tell you a little story about my good friend and former roommate, Jay. As a newly minted American from Turkey, I always found Jay to be wonderfully positive about many things those of us born here whine about.

He's just so damn appreciative of being here and chasing the dream, it is truly inspiring.

In one of our many late-night conversations in the kitchen, Jay and I spoke earnestly about work ethic and the need to 'do what you've got to do' to get ahead in life. We both started working in our early teens, and neither of us held the belief that we were 'too good' for hard work–or, as we decided to call it, "Digging Your Ditches." We'd pass each other in the living room or the hallway and ask, "How are you doing, my friend?"

Inevitably, the answer was something like, "Digging my ditches!" and we'd exchange a look of mutual respect.

Back then, we each worked more than 12 hours per day. I had my day job and fledgling coaching business; Jay had his production company, and to send money home to Mom, was also driving Uber.

After a particularly tough year in my business and a failed program launch, I went through a sort of 'dark night of the soul.' where I struggled with questions about what I was meant to do, who I was meant to serve, and why no matter what I did, I felt blocked from moving forward.

By this time, I had gotten enough education and done enough deep inner work to know that trying to force an answer wouldn't create the progress I sought; of course, being a stubborn Leo, I tried anyway. *Doing* is what we driven women do best, after all.

Finally, after an insightful conversation with my own coach, I decided I needed to step back from my business for a beat and let the dust (and my wallet) settle.

And so—I decided it was time to dig some different ditches. After consulting Jay, I chose to spend some time driving Uber as well. The idea was to drive nights and fill my coffers so I could take myself on a travel retreat. Some of my best seasons had followed a solo adventure, and I was eager for the inspiration and healing.

I've got to be honest here and tell you that once I was on the road for a bit, and the novelty wore off, it really felt like a step backward.

I thought about how busting my butt for around $10 an hour (after taxes and gas) was beneath me. I made great money at the day job and was emerging into high fees as a coach.

No one talks about the investment required to be an entrepreneur, and few business coaches get real about the investment needed to launch a program.

Truth bomb: Being what I call a Femmepreneur is both expensive and challenging, far beyond what most talk about in the feed.

And so, as a driver, I had ultimate flexibility with very little investment and, honestly, a small reward for the time investment. On many late nights, I quietly questioned whether or not it was worth it. I was so damn tired. But, I was also glad to side-hustle up the money to travel.

I began to realize, though, that this little night job of mine helped me see several things differently.

First, my relationship with my money became much more passionate, and I learned to appreciate it more than I had in a very long time. As I contemplated purchases, I considered how many rides it would take to recoup those dollars.

Yes, I know all about abundance thinking and manifestation, but I'm here to tell you that loving your money by appreciating it does, in fact, create more abundance. I don't think it's good to waste or throw away energy. And money is energy.

I also learned to trust the Universe again. It began with little requests to snag a good fare or end the night with a ride that took me close to home.

I soon returned to my former levels of faith, trust, and pixie dust.

This little hustle also afforded the coach in me many opportunities to help people. It felt so good to give back to those who clearly needed and wanted 20-30 minutes of high-level coaching. They'd leave my car with insight and a baby step.

I began to trust in my abilities as a coach again. My tough year had really put a dent in my self-image.

And then, one day, the Universe showed me exactly why this temporary job was so important:

I picked up a woman from her work and started driving her home. It was a 25-minute ride, so we settled into chatting. We saw a homeless man talking to himself, and we both commented that it was such a shame. My passenger said he was probably high, too, and then she mentioned that her husband sometimes talked to himself, as he was currently struggling with a methamphetamine addiction. Having been close to at least one person who went through meth addiction, I shook my head sorrowfully and expressed empathy.

I said, "It's so hard to watch someone you care about get so lost."

What ensued was 10 minutes of her crying about his physical abuse—on her and her children. She explained that he'd call her at work, accuse her of having an affair, and then 'punish' her when she got home. At this moment, she was terrified of how her night would go.

I did something a coach should never do. And something I never thought I would do, having been there myself. I flat-out told her to leave. And then I told her the story of the day my friends dared to have an intervention.

I told her how impossible it seemed for me to leave him back then, how I owned the company and had a house full of furniture, a dog, and my son staying with me. I explained my fears about starting over with nothing and my hopes that he would somehow change.

I was honest with her about how tough it was to start over with nothing– and how it had taken years to find my feet again.

She nodded in understanding, and I could see her gearing up to tell me these were the reasons she would stay.

But then I told her about the day I realized that if I didn't leave, I would soon be dead.

I will never forget the look on her face when I said that. Her whole body went still, and she looked solemnly into my rearview mirror at me with her big, dark eyes. This was her moment, just like when I had that moment.

There was no denying the singular truth that if she stayed, *she* believed there was a good chance that she would not survive.

We ended with a tender moment in the car, where I reached back and took her hand.

I said, "Listen, no matter what you decide to do, know this: You are not an accident. You are valuable. You have a purpose, and it isn't to be someone's punching bag."

She squeezed my hand, wiped the tears from her eyes, thanked me, and got out of the car.

I still think of her often and hope she did leave. I hope she started again and that she and her children are now safe. I do know with all my heart that I was supposed to be her driver that day.

And this is where I tell you that digging your ditches isn't always about you. Sometimes, it is about the journey, which is why those in the know about abundance and manifestation talk so much about not being attached to the outcome.

But sometimes, digging ditches becomes about someone else. My three and a half months of driving was about something other than the money for travel.

Even when we struggle to find the rainbow in the storm, our highest self has a way of using our intuition to direct us toward what we–or someone else needs, even while we're questioning it.

What are your thoughts about the stories I've told you? Do you relate in any way?

What are your 'digging ditches' stories?

I want to say now that I totally get it that many women have not been through the challenges I've described so far, but I'd like you to know that there are things I have seen, experienced, and survived that have made me a badass coach.

That is not to say that a good coach should have my background; instead, I insist that I am a better coach because of it.

I was the first in my family to graduate from college. There are a few of us now, but I'm still the only one with two master's degrees. I've come a long way, baby. That said, one of the most valuable lessons I have learned is that I don't have to be the smartest person in the room. And when I am coaching my incredible clients, I am definitely not the smartest person in the room.

So, while I am here to share my research, my experiences, and those of my clients, I don't claim to be some sort of guru; I am merely here to provide a bit of insight. Any related work will be up to you.

And it will be work.

Some years ago, I read a book review on Amazon where the reader complained that they couldn't relate to the stories about 'that day at yoga class' and similar stories shared by the author. She was describing a middle to upper-class experience. And it is entirely possible that some of the experiences I share here won't be relatable to all readers. The thing is, we're all women.

I have seen many shades of poverty and wealth. When I was being mentally abused by my husband, I was treated as a millionaire, even though most of the wealth was his and not mine. People treated me very differently than when I didn't have that lifestyle.

I have also been homeless, with nowhere to go. I know what it means to be at rock bottom.

All this is to say that one woman's ditches aren't meant to be compared to another's. Not all stories and experiences are entirely relatable; however, I believe there are great nuggets of insight if you look for them.

I'd like to ask you now to look for them here in this book.

Digging ditches doesn't have to mean hustling at a second job. It can be a way of being–a way of showing up, not being afraid to grab that shovel, and just. dig. in.

This sense of the term is not about working harder. As driven women, we all know how to do that. I'm talking about the bravery of daring to challenge yourself–daring to trust in yourself and your talents. Maybe, even daring to:

Write that book
Start a new company
Speak up for yourself
Negotiate for a higher position or salary

There are so many other things that require the digging of ditches. Let me tell you about one that may surprise you:

Rosa came to me as a CEO, ready for a new season. Or so she claimed in our first session when she said, "I just want to get a little piece of heaven for myself and slow down. I want to retire. I can afford it; why not retire at 50?"

Fifty was the following year. And we'll get into this more later, but the thing about 'tomorrow' or 'next year' is that our brain literally sees this as it would a perfect stranger.

In other words, tomorrow or next year have no damn relevance for us. That's why it is so easy to put things off!

When Rosa thought of retiring 'next year,' it held no real threat until I suggested she start a viable plan. I had her jot down three questions to contemplate for our next session:

- What would you have to let go of to get serious about retirement next year?

- Write a day in the life of your retirement. What does it look and feel like?

- Make a quick action list, and then take the first baby step toward your retirement this week.

As Rosa wrote down my questions, I could see her face change. She began smoothing her dark hair with her hand; next, she took brief breaks and bit her lower lip. The stress response was palpable, even through Zoom.

I asked Rosa to take a beat and do some diaphragmatic breathing with me. These simple 'belly breaths' slow down our heart rate, mind, and breathing.

Immediately, I could see Rosa begin to calm, and when we resumed our chat, I asked her what she had been feeling and thinking.

"Oh my God, I'm not ready to retire," Rosa almost yelled, "What was I thinking!"

At this moment, next year was banging on the door with a suitcase, and Rosa was not ready for this abrupt shift from perfect stranger to roommate. The panic was so unsettling that she was prepared to put her dream away.

For Rosa, digging ditches wasn't planning her retirement. For Rosa, digging ditches was the act of slowing down–in her mind, preparing to do 'nothing.'

For a driven woman, the mere concept of stillness can be terrifying. This brings us back to the layers of programming.

For Rosa and for many of us, keeping 'busy' is our way of keeping ourselves out of our trauma. And so the idea of stillness can put us into fight or flight mode, stimulating an amygdala hijack.

If Rosa became still, there would be time to consider her marriage, which was having some challenges.

Wait. Her challenged marriage was trauma? Yes. It was. Somewhere in her mind, Rosa's challenged marriage equaled the danger of failure, and failure wasn't an option. Of course, this belief had to do with several of her other experiences, from her childhood as the daughter of an Army captain to her time on the drafting table at her firm, where she was now CEO.

The connection Rosa made between her feelings of panic about having stillness in her life and possibly failing at her marriage may have been realized in that first session, but it was weeks before the core belief emerged.

In the following weeks, I had Rosa do some work with her subconscious, or what I call our inner supervillain.

— THREE —

The Inner Supervillain

When I developed the idea of our subconscious being the Inner Supervillain, I was in the depths of my struggle to heal from that last abusive marriage. I had gone through quite a lot, having moved across the country with my son and my little chihuahua; first, to my Auntie's home in Washington, then in just two weeks, the move to our apartment and a new job in Texas, and after 18 months there, my son was finally in treatment at a mental wellness facility in Ohio. Whew!

Thank you to my son's Grandma and Grandpa!

I was alone for the first time in many years. And that is when it hit me. I had never really taken the time to heal. I was so focused on the move, the job, and shlepping my son to therapy that I hadn't taken a beat for myself.

The night I returned home from taking my son to Ohio, I cried with such relief and fear it shocked me.

This is Driven Woman Syndrome at its finest. Surrounded by things to do and take care of, I had let eighteen months elapse without ever really healing. Later, I realized I could have quite easily continued to avoid my trauma for years to come, but somehow, my healing began just a handful of weeks later.

This next part is hard to get into. Partly because it is painful and complicated and also because while I want to share some of my stories with you, this book is not my memoir. So, I'll keep it short:

I was essentially homeless at this point. I had a job. I always had a job. But in trying to care for my son before his grandparents stepped in, I had buried myself financially, emotionally, and physically. I really needed to relocate and downsize so I could begin to recover.

These wonderful friends offered me their spare room for one month. I jumped on the offer and immediately started packing and planning my move back to California. Within days of my arrival, I began an earnest job hunt, and four weeks to the day later, I landed a terrific job as a Director and found a sweet little cottage for me and my dog to live in.

Finally, in that tiny cottage, I knew it was time to face myself. This one question had been plaguing me for years.

How did a strong, driven, successful woman like me keep ending up in those abusive relationships?

It is surprising to some people that I didn't know the answer. I used to joke that when I did find out, I'd write a book about it.

And so, here I am, writing a book not just about the answer but the things I learned along the way about myself, other 'strong, driven, successful' women like me, and something I now call Driven Woman Syndrome. Based on my research, I make an assertion that in part references the work of Steven N. Gold, Ph.D., psychiatrist Judith Herman, and others. Here's the short version:

Those of us who suffered Adverse Childhood Experiences as children, who also learned that pleasing, performing, and perfecting behaviors 'kept the peace' or, as a result of these behaviors, sometimes experienced what felt like approval and acceptance, were often denied fundamental interpersonal resources that children need.

The lack of these resources cemented core beliefs behind the behaviors, and as we continued to grow up, pleasing, performing, and perfecting habits were rewarded by our culturescape. We were often encouraged and described as strong, competitive, enterprising, adaptive, supportive, driven, capable, hard-working, steadfast, diligent, peace-keeping perfectionists.

Think about how often you have heard, "You're so strong!" or "You're so organized!"

Behind that strength and organization is the voice. That former child, now woman in our mind who pushes, criticizes, and makes mostly inaccurate statements about us and our environment that move us forward but also cause stress and anxiety. Because that voice also seems to keep us safe, we tolerate her.

Frequently, that voice is protecting us from the trauma related to Adverse Childhood Experiences.

For the sake of clarity, as we continue, I will define a couple of terms:

Trauma is when a person perceives an event or set of circumstances as frightening, harmful, or threatening, whether emotionally, physically, or both. With trauma, a child's experience of strong negative emotions and physiological symptoms (e.g., rapid heartbeat, bedwetting, stomach aches) may develop soon afterward and continue well beyond their initial exposure.

Adverse Childhood Experiences (ACEs), a term coined by researchers Vincent Felitti, Robert Anda, and colleagues in their study conducted from 1995 to 1997–are a subset of childhood adversities. According to the CDC, 61% of adults in 25 states reported they had experienced at least one type of ACE before age 18, and nearly 1 in 6 said they had experienced four or more types of adverse childhood experiences. Traumatic events that can have lasting negative effects range from having a loved one attempt or die by suicide, experiencing or witnessing violence, being abused or neglected, growing up in a household where parents were separated or in jail, doing drugs, or having mental health issues. Although ACEs can be prevented, sadly, they are common occurrences for many children.

With that out of the way, let me tell you how I came up with the analogy that the woman's voice in our head is our Inner Supervillain. I'd like you to imagine her as you recall your favorite female supervillain:

She suffered trauma as a kid. And then more trauma as an adult. Along the way, she begins to hold inaccurate core beliefs that inform her choices. She hides her pain behind a mask. She doesn't know the truth from the lies of the stories she tells herself about both past and current experiences, particularly regarding her self-worth. Sometimes, she gets close to a breakthrough, but she's constantly collecting evidence to prove the stories she's accepted as fact. Pain is bad, so she generally avoids it–which sometimes causes it. Pleasure is good, which she always prefers–but sometimes causes pain. And she's always got something to prove; if not to the world, then certainly to herself. She needs a win. And she must show she is capable of what others claim she isn't.

See? That voice–our subconscious, *is* our Inner Supervillain. She's sassy, intelligent, and lovable in many ways. While she may be driven and capable, her choices aren't always best for her, but her vulnerability makes you want to hug her tight and help her figure it out.

And that is how we *should* treat her.

Her ability to block stuff she doesn't want to deal with and be a badass is almost inspiring. *Almost.*

Blocking the 'bad' stuff actually fosters inaccurate core beliefs and prevents us from fully knowing ourselves. The Inner Supervillain effectively buries our traumatic moments deep in a cave somewhere and attempts to keep us safe by doing so. Why do I keep saying *she*? Because *she* isn't *you*. Instead, she is the sum total of all of the experiences of your five senses since you jumped into this suit you call a human being.

The part of us that dreams and goes somewhere when we leave this earth is a *different* us. Maybe with the memories of our subconscious mind but adrift of this world, it's definitely something else. A piece of our soul, perhaps. Play with me on this. It's an analogy that has helped many clients over the years. And it still helps me.

abits

Here's an easy-to-try, easy-to-do set of habits that changed my life and that of my clients:

- Think of your inner supervillain. Design her. What does she look like? What's her name?

- What three things has she done lately that don't serve you? e.g., saying statements around the core belief that "I am unworthy, unloved," or "undeserving."

- Next time you hear *her voice* talking to yourself, talk back! Say this:
  I appreciate that you are having some feelings, but these sorts of statements don't' serve us, and I don't have time for them, okay? If you still want to talk about it on Sunday at 3pm, see you then.

- One thing I did when I first started doing this was to track how many times a day I needed to chat with her. On many days, the number (that I bothered to track) was over 30! That is at least 30 times *per day* that I was saying really shitty, unhelpful things to myself!

- Actually make time for her on Sunday at 3pm, or whatever time you choose. Get out a piece of paper and write the following:
  Hi! Glad to see you. I promised you could chat about those feelings you wanted to talk about. Ready? Go! And give her 30 seconds to write down as many doubts, fears, and concerns as she can. Then, stop.

- Go back and read what she wrote. Ask yourself how accurate it seems. Or is it based on predicted outcomes based on past experiences or stories?

    Then I usually write something like:

    Thank you so much for sharing this with me. I hear you. But I want you to know you are safe, and I've got this. I am totally ready to _____ and know you will have my back, and please know that I have yours. (invisible hug).

Give it a go and see how it feels. It's been about nine years, and I still practice these habits.

Here's why it works psychologically: It removes you from the shit talk and stories just enough to allow some emotional distance.

Having some distance provides opportunities to question the habits, behaviors, attitudes, and beliefs that make up these statements we repeat subconsciously to ourselves over and over and over, essentially brainwashing ourselves into an autopilot that just doesn't serve us.

Stepping outside of the autopilot and into our conscious mind allows us to *choose* what we move forward with rather than knee-jerk respond to things.

There's more to it than this, but starting to get your subconscious comfortable with *you* taking the lead is a terrific first step. Think about how many things you respond to without questioning whether you a) believe the story going on inside your head or b) actually want to respond this way.

The more we challenge our thinking patterns, the more control and choice we have over what we allow ourselves to respond to, how we want to respond, or *if* we want to respond.

Additionally, when our subconscious gains trust in our more conscious lead, she learns to hesitate and listen to our purposeful, intentional thinking patterns. And that is good for us. I make her sound like her own personality, don't I? If you think about it, our subconscious is her own personality. According to Science, She rules our world 95% of the time.

I sometimes get odd looks when I first introduce the concept of the Inner Supervillain at speaking engagements; however, the subconscious is very real no matter how you frame it and, left unchecked, can seriously wreak havoc on our lives.

So, hey—It is time to circle back to the discussion of *allowing* our experiences to *count*.

There is no threshold for what should qualify as trauma. For some children, a divorce or a move is deeply traumatic. For others, it is a myriad of other events and experiences. And it is imperative not to dismiss symptoms of trauma that lasted more than three months after the initial event, as that is classified as PTSD.

Of course, not all trauma leads to PTSD, and not all PTSD requires treatment. But if a child who experiences Post Traumatic Stress Disorder needs care and remains untreated, they can experience life-long issues, such as anxiety, depression, and more.

I remind you of some truths around trauma just in case you didn't see yourself in the definitions provided and you're doing that thing we do where we read the word 'trauma' and immediately think, "Oh, that's for other people."

Yvonne thought trauma was for other people. She had heard of me through a friend at my day job, where I was a Director. I mainly coached one or two clients on Saturdays while earning my second coaching certification and was happy to take on a third client to gain more experience and hours.

These sessions were in person in her classroom. We had the entire school to ourselves, except for the band that could be heard practicing on the field. Being a former teacher myself, I felt right at home.

What Yvonne couldn't understand, she explained, was why she was so anxious all the time. She had a pretty great life.

It had gotten really bad on her recent honeymoon trip to Bora Bora. She and her husband Derrick had decided to go on a diving excursion. They fell in love with the experience and decided to enroll in the resort's certification program, and the plan was to dive every day for five days.

On the day of conducting a 30-foot dive that included a task called "mask clearing," Yvonne and Derrick jumped excitedly into the boat and began performing the various equipment-check steps.

As Yvonne recalled the event, her voice began to tremble, and she asked if she could stand as she finished the story.

I asked Yvonne if she was okay to continue, and she nodded. "Here is what's weird," she explained, "I had already done this exercise in the pool. But for some reason, I completely panicked when we got down to the ocean floor."

Yvonne began to pace around the front of her classroom, stopping at the podium. There, Yvonne seemed to find her calm. She asked if I minded if she stayed there. I understood immediately that this space, specifically this podium, helped her to feel more comfortable. Of course, I didn't mind at all. She gripped the slanted wooden top with both hands and finished her story.

The long and short of it was that she needed to be rescued from the ocean floor by the dive master before she could even begin the exercise, and to make matters worse, she couldn't get back into the water at all after that.

"Derrick was so upset," Yvonne concluded, "but I just couldn't do it. Since then, I can't even talk about diving again without crying."

From Yvonne's perspective, she ruined their honeymoon over a random stupid incident. And then she told me that she didn't understand why this bothered her so much. After all, her dad had died thirty years prior, and she had been in the ocean many times since.

I politely interrupted with, "If you're comfortable, please share about your dad."

When Yvonne was six, her dad had been doing work on the river. To maintain her privacy, I'll simply state there was a very publicized accident.

Yvonne's dad had died that day, and rescue divers had struggled to recover his body. It had been on the news and in the papers. As far as Yvonne was concerned, this was a completely unrelated experience. Because she was only six then, she didn't feel her father's sudden death *qualified* as a traumatic experience.

There had never been therapy, but she did remember that she didn't speak for several weeks afterward, and in second grade, she had gone to a speech therapist at school for a stutter.

Only at that moment did she make the connection.

Not only did Yvonne experience trauma at the loss of her father, but she had many symptoms for over a year following his death.

We didn't swim into the deep end of that trauma; Yvonne didn't need to relive the experience with me. Instead, it was important to be aware that there was trauma, recognize the connection, and give herself some compassion and acceptance.

In (and outside) the following sessions, Yvonne did some work around navigating stress and anxiety and also spent time journaling each week with her Inner Supervillain.

Along the way, she discovered that there were several related struggles she had experienced and was able to find context and closure around those difficult times.

We worked together for six months but stayed in touch afterward. The couple returned to Tahiti for their second anniversary and completed their Open Water certification. The last time we spoke, Yvonne talked about some version of retirement where she and Derrick could go diving every day.

All of this sounds pretty idyllic, right? A client sees me for six months and leaves with an exciting new life. In this case, that is partly true. But there is more, and I don't want to mislead anyone here.

Yvonne was willing to do the deep inner work. She became even more committed to our weekly sessions and, on our week off each month, carving out time to do things such as journaling, meditating, exercising, being considerate of what she ate, going on long reflective walks, and more.

Our time together did not create instant change, and Yvonne is an incredibly driven woman. Carving out this time was a challenging task.

Initially, she tried to create a daily schedule that incorporated these things. What resulted was not pretty.

Her daily planner was packed from 5am until midnight, carefully and meticulously arranged so she could have time for self-care activities and not neglect a single person or project. Needless to say, this was not sustainable.

At one point, the tension between her and Derrick was so intense that Yvonne questioned if their love was real or strong enough to sustain them while she went through this work. She even considered taking a break from the relationship as the pressure of working on her new marriage, and herself competed with her career for her time.

Rather than blow up her life, I suggested that perhaps she take a look at many irons in her fire and reevaluate.

Initially, Yvonne could not imagine removing a single thing from her priority list.

After some conversation and reflection, however, she realized that for almost a year, she had said yes to every request that crossed her desk. Being a dedicated educator, she always stayed late, always took work home, and served on several committees, as well as coming in on week-ends to be an assistant coach to the robotics team.

At this point, she realized something needed to change. So we played the hell-yes game.

We reviewed every item in her planner for a month, and she got to circle the items with a blue pen that made her feel a resounding "Hell yes!"

Everything else became suspect and put on the table for possible evaluation.

There were justifications, explanations, and some tough compromises. In the end, Yvonne had a schedule that made her feel satisfied without completely draining her resources.

Learning to pause and say no was yet another challenge, but that, too, became a skill in her self-care portfolio.

Yvonne had struggled with meeting her own expectations and experienced the roller-coaster of falling and getting back up that comes with doing this work. There were days she wanted to quit altogether. On one such occasion, she proclaimed, "It's easier to stay in the cave!"

— FOUR —

Shadow Work Or The League of Villains

Before I heard the term 'shadow work.' I had already spoken to my daughter about a concept I was working on. When I described it and showed her the illustration below, she nodded and said, "You should call them the League of Villains."

The idea that came to me was derived partly from an ancient text I used in my High School English classroom in the early 2000s called Plato's Allegory of the Cave.

Here is a loose synopsis: There are these prisoners who are chained inside of a cave. They can't move their heads around to look behind them, nor can they get up and generally look around.

They are forced to look at the cave wall, where shadows are cast upon it by a fire and people walking between this fire and the prisoners on a long walkway. It's basically a live puppet show.

The prisoners never know what anything actually looks like, or to put it another way, they never understand reality the way the Philosopher King can do, which, in part, is Plato's point. Restricted to only one point of view, these poor prisoners never know true light or any object being carried on the walkway.

One day, a prisoner breaks free and goes out into the world. *Light! Real things!* She is amazed and enraptured with the truth.

The prisoner runs back to the cave to share her joy. She wants to free the remaining prisoners from their shackles and lack of enlightenment.

See how this works for the Philosopher King?

Or not, as the prisoners become enraged and proceed to kill the enlightened messenger.

One of the many lessons of this allegory is that we humans get so stuck in our own stories that we don't always want to know the truth. In fact, should someone come along and shatter our perceptions of what is and isn't, we can become angry, lost in denial, and quite stubborn.

It is such a great allegory and easy to relate to, right? Up to the day of graduation and well beyond, many of my students would come back to visit me and tell me a story of how someone they knew was stuck in their cave.

We always see *others* as the prisoner.

Years later, while doing my deep inner work, I thought of how we have these 'selves' (or what they call 'parts' in psychology) that represent sort of trauma snapshots:

- That six-year-old who still feels shame.

- The ten-year-old with depression who got bullied.

- The sixteen-year-old who feels ignored and can't get past the divorce.

- The twenty-two-year-old who lost a parent too young.

In my analogy-ridden mind, these snapshot versions of us are individual villains with detailed stories wrapped around these trauma snapshots. They hang out in their secret League of Villains cave with the Inner Supervillain, who acts as their leader and enables them by helping them to collect evidence to support their stories.

Because our subconscious runs the show, we become much like the prisoner, accepting the shadows on the wall as our reality, buying into her whispered stories, half-truths, and downright lies.

I know I'm being cheeky here, but seriously—do you really want to be the prisoner of your own subconscious?

There are two difficult questions here:

- How do we become more conscious?

- What is real, anyway?

Of course, we can ask a more philosophical twister: If it feels real to me, isn't it entirely real?

To that, I respond with Hell, yes, it does. And that's the problem. All emotions feel real. And so they are real. But I invite you to ask yourself, *Is the narrative behind the feelings accurate?*

Carl Jung's shadow archetype is described as the "dark, emotional, immoral," and even "inferior" parts of our psyche. Examples are long-standing characters such as Dracula, dragons, or other destructors. What's interesting to me about this view is that it correlates with how *we see* our own villains. More often than not, these psychological snapshots bring us shame and embarrassment or trigger other undesirable emotions.

Our autopilot-subconscious, or Inner Supervillain, then serves us (she thinks) by keeping them hidden away from view. Unfortunately, this protective mechanism only supports the 'story' that we should feel shame around these villains.

The result is that we can grow into our 40s, as I did, without truly facing these villains or, in other cases, not knowing these villains exist at all. The outcome of which is a powder keg of a triggerfest waiting to happen.

The truth is, we aren't really encouraged to be that self-aware. We certainly aren't trained to befriend our villains/Jung's shadow archetype.

That brings us to shadow work, which correlates nicely with my villain analogy, a generalization of Jung's archetype, and also Parts Work, which we'll get to shortly.

Shadow Work is often associated with Jung's work, but with more research, it seems to differ slightly in how one views the shadow.

While Jung's description of the shadow almost literally demonizes our shadow (another popular character comparison is the Devil), the idea of conducting Shadow Work, coined by Ivan Illich in his 1981 book of the same title, takes a softer, more spiritual approach alongside therapy.

Parts Work is definitely a bit more current and has a 'reintegration' focus, which, in this coach's opinion, is much more desirable than shaming our villains or picking at their wounds.

By observing, listening to, and befriending our villains, we can also support them to be more comfortable with being observed and coached.

I know; I'm doing that thing again where I treat these 'characters' as though they are real. Yep. Because I know both as a coach and firsthand what ignoring our subconscious does. And these 'parts,' or our 'Shadow Self' or, as I prefer it, 'League of Villains,' need our *conscious* attention so that we can live healthier, fuller lives.

Here's how I put my analogies together: I think of the League of Villains as these various snapshots of emotional trauma. They turn to our Inner Supervillain to protect them and keep them hidden because they're undesirable, unwelcome, and seen as monsters. Our subconscious is happy to help. After all, it is her job to keep us safe.

Building up trust with our Inner Supervillain, then, allows us to have a deeper awareness of the members of the League. Getting to a place of curiosity and observation is the goal. It helps us become less triggered and more aware.

Becoming more aware helps us connect with our core beliefs and make decisions about our values, which in turn help us to make informed choices that align with our whole self–without the mask of the habits of pleasing, performing, and perfecting. While those habits are instilled early and consistently reinforced throughout our lives, teaching our subconscious different behavior patterns is possible.

Remember Yvonne, my client who discovered her six-year-old villain had decided to crash her honeymoon?

It was the work of observation that led her to so many breakthroughs about the impact her father's death had on her, not just as a six-year-old but throughout her entire life. Learning techniques and practicing supportive habits that allowed her to quickly reestablish calm and observe the moment helped her *allow* feelings to emerge that she could view, question, and analyze without the former Amygdala hijack experience of panic and anxiety.

Over time (and it did take time), she became more comfortable lengthening these exchanges with her Inner Supervillain. As trust was built, she could reframe beliefs she was unaware of. Yvonne experienced the freedom to be whole. In six months? No. It is a lifetime journey, to be sure; however, the Yvonne I spoke to last was a very different, much more confident woman than the one I met that day in her classroom.

I am convinced that with continued practice, Yvonne will live a wonderful, fulfilling life where she is the director of her movie and where the League of Villains doesn't need to be kept in a cave somewhere by her Inner Supervillain.

The first time these techniques make a difference, it changes everything. Then, it becomes a matter of working at it every day for consistency. But make no mistake: Befriending your subconscious does work. The alternative is not ideal because when I say our subconscious rules our world 95% of the time, that is Science. New habits take time and practice.

Now is an excellent time to say that working with trauma has its challenges–and some of those challenges require a very good therapist who has experience in working with trauma.

Depending on the situation and client, I readily make referrals, or if my client prefers, I can work in tandem with their therapist. If you find yourself feeling remotely shaken by this work, please don't hesitate to consult a therapist, trauma-informed coach, or both. Seriously. You don't have to do this work alone. Asking for help is a good thing.

Even after years of doing this work, I still have to practice staying unshakable. And to be clear, being unshakable doesn't mean we don't *ever* freak out, cry, get angry, or have pity parties. It does mean that, more often than not, we are more measured, more thoughtful, and more at ease with ourselves and our feelings.

One of my favorite examples for myself happened just last year. I'll share it because It is a good illustration of what the experience of allowing and observing can entail. This story is also pretty 'woo'.

I was watching television. I would love to say it was PBS or some other high-quality show, which I do enjoy–but on this day, it was crappy reality television. The person being interviewed said something about constantly feeling like an outsider, as though they never belonged at all.

Something about this statement of isolation and feeling 'other' triggered my Inner Supervillain so intensely that my body responded before I was even aware of it.

I lept off the couch and into my kitchen, where I began opening and closing drawers as though there was an urgent task to complete. As I opened the third drawer, I realized there was nothing I needed to do in the kitchen.

I said to my Inner Supervillain, "Hold on. Let's just be still for a moment." I grabbed the edges of my kitchen island and forced my body to stay put.

I did a technique I'll talk more about later. I call it "Droning." I closed my eyes, imagined I was on my ceiling, looking down at myself, and began observing. Out loud, I said, "Hmm, isn't that interesting," as I took inventory of what had just occurred. I had just heard someone else make a statement about a feeling I clearly identified with in some way.

First question: Is this feeling mine to own?

No. But there's a trigger here.

Second question: Where in the body is this trigger located?

My hands released the island and immediately rose to my heart.

Not a question–A directive. Let's breathe.

Slowly, hands still on my heart, I began to do my diaphragmatic breathing. 8 counts in–then hold 4, 3, 2, 1, and then 8 counts out.

Good. If this isn't my feeling to own, and it is heart-centered, what is this about?

Between my breaths, I heard myself say my son's name. I realized I had been thinking a lot about him lately, making connections between us and other, more distant relatives, one of whom I also felt very connected to.

"This isn't even my shit," I exclaimed, "It's DNA, family shit."

I caught the impulse to sweep it aside or, more accurately, under.

Hold on. Stay put. What are these feelings? Let's allow them to come.

Tears were already streaming down my face. I automatically began to pace in circles around my kitchen island, and then the sobs started. I wanted to find something to do.

Not yet. Give it just a little longer. Breathe.

I breathed. And I cried. I closed my eyes again and stood still. That is when the insight came.

My subconscious had made a connection between this ancestor, myself, and my son. I always felt a weird connection to this ancestor–one I still can't fully explain. This ancestry of mine had a very difficult life. She had been in at least one abusive marriage and lost her children in a very violent way. Just five years later, she married a second time, and when her third child was just eleven or twelve, she was admitted into an asylum, where she died soon after.

Knowing some of my story, the reason this woman's life would touch me is not surprising. But the connection, I feel, is more than that. Again, I can't really explain it–it is just there.

My son's story is its own book, but I will simply say that he is lost to me, and his mental health is lost to him.

The intensity of the 'otherness' that they both must have experienced in their lives awakens a deep empathy and compassion–and, though I'd like to deny it, a recognition.

I know intimately the experience of feeling like an outsider. And watching my son struggle with that experience has been deeply painful, mainly because while he had his challenges, he was also highly brilliant. And, of course, watching him struggle also gave me pause to question my own mental health over the years, particularly when each of my husbands tried to gaslight me with claims of my being 'crazy.'

Discovering the background of a relative who landed in an asylum didn't exactly build a castle of confidence either.

Thankfully, I have done a good amount of research and work with children and adults with a history of trauma, ACEs, and those on the spectrum. This work and study have given me much insight into our mental health system in this country.

Unfortunately, my opinions about our system are not kind. And the way our culturescape views mental health is only just evolving.

We have a very long way to go, and in my opinion, our state facilities are still genuinely terrifying. I have seen firsthand how readily strong, brain-altering drugs are administered–and I've also witnessed how (due to severe underfunding and understaffing) people who need serious care are simply released onto the street under the most minimum of requirements.

I share all of this because it is relevant to my jumping off the couch that day and because I think it's essential to be part of the solution for a seriously detrimental stigma surrounding mental health.

And so, my very intense reaction that day that seemed to come from nowhere definitely came from somewhere.

I've come to understand that not only do I feel connected to my son and distant relative's plight, but my own experiences with mental abuse have a lot of old, complex programming attached. Being told consistently for so many years that something was wrong with me is still a deep trigger point. And while I very much want to say that all of my deep inner work has completely healed that trauma, the truth is that those villains are still part of my journey.

What has changed is that now, when these triggers emerge, I no longer hide from them. If I have the time and space, I face them in the moment. Should that not be the case, I make an appointment with myself to do the work.

Well, that was a lot to share. Part of me wants to delete these words and give you a different, less vulnerable story. Instead, I will trust that someone needs to read the truth.

Over the years, I have read some fantastic books that provided me with great insight; however, invariably, there comes the moment when we ask, "But how do I actually do what you're describing?"

The answer is almost always the same: Habits. Sure, there is much more—but getting started with some habits makes all the difference.

We have talked about getting started with your Inner Supervillain, and that habit takes time. First, you've got to catch her in the act, usually talking shit or making statements related to not being enough of some-thing.

Then, it is about cutting her off and letting her know that while now isn't the time for that conversation about her fears, concerns, and doubts, Sunday at 3pm (or whatever time you decide works best) is when she will have the chance to let it all hang out—with limits.

And like a good therapist or coach, you will provide your Inner Supervil-lain with a safe space to share and encourage her to investigate whether her stories are accurate or helpful.

You will conclude with a loving assertion that you are the most capable of leading and that with her incredible talents, great things are possible!

It may seem silly that you have to earn the trust of a part of yourself, but your subconscious doesn't trust you for good reasons. Remember when she had to stop the car, respond to the burning smell, or some other life-saving moment?

We must remember that our Inner Supervillain is not something we need to conquer, beat, or otherwise win over.

Keeping you safe is literally her job. So remember to respect, appreciate, and honor her for it.

The next step is to slowly welcome the presence of the League of Villains–or your shadow self–or your parts. Whatever works for you.

Habits

You may not yet be ready for these habits, which is fine. That is why I reminded you about beginning to notice what your Inner Supervillain is up to so you can establish that trust.

But when you are ready, here is a habit you can try to incorporate into your weekly chat:

Ask her to focus on this topic: What is currently holding me back?

Stretch her time to share to one minute. If that goes well, increase the time, with two minutes as the hard limit. Then, read it back to yourself with a quiet offer of encouragement.

Breathe. I like good diaphragmatic breathing: an 8-second belly breath in, followed by a 4-second hold, then an 8-second breath out where your navel presses in toward your spine.

Make your offer: Is there anything in this writing that needs to be briefly unpacked or discussed?

Remind your subconscious that this is a safe space, and it is just you, her, and any villains that may want to chat. Keep breathing. Close your eyes.

To be clear: This is not a deep dive excavation of piles of yucky shit! This should merely be a gentle questioning–asking if there might be something holding you back that needs a little examination or discussion.

Ask if there is someplace in your body where this thing, whatever it may be, resides.

Some common locations are the neck and/or shoulders, ankles or knees, lower back, heart, and others.

After extensive work with my clients on these issues, I have come to rely on two fantastic books by Evette Rose. The chart I've assembled below is constructed using a mix of her concepts from Metaphysical Anatomy and confirmations from my clients' personal experiences. As a certified Emotion Code® and Body Code® practitioner, I rely heavily on one of my mentors, Dr. Bradley Nelson, in this work as well.

It is only a tiny sample of the breadth of work possible in considering how the body speaks to us, but it can be helpful in this context to suss out residual issues going on as you work with your Inner Supervillain.

In your questioning, ask, "Is there a place in my body where emotions and beliefs are residing that may be holding me back?" Go with your first, up to five-second response, as that is where our intuition lives. Here is a brief chart to help you consider those six most common locations:

Location	Emotions	Consider
Neck	Need to fix or lack of control	Resistance or avoidance - feeling controlled
Shoulders	Weighed down but still willing to take on more. Carrying burdens of others.	Trust or self-esteem - need permission to be powerful
Ankles	The future, lack of control, conflict with mother	Flexibility related to future, stubbornness
Knees	Stuck. No actionable plan to move forward on project or personal	New season, held back by expectations
Lower back	Financial - possibly burdened, peacekeeper	Acceptance, fear of failure
Heart	Lack of expression, regret, resentment, control	Expressing feelings, emotions, worthiness

These are meant to be starting points for your consideration as you attempt to dial into your subconscious and its body expressions. The chart is not comprehensive or complete, but you may find it a helpful first step in considering how your subconscious may be holding on to feelings and how, by simply asking, you can understand some of these subtle communications.

Remember, your subconscious has a primary directive to protect you and doesn't understand the ramifications of hiding these feelings. Gratitude for the trust given can go a long way, even if it feels weird or sounds silly.

When you're ready, give it a go. See what comes up for you. Remember to breathe.

— FIVE —

Voice

This topic is a big one for me. When I was a child, I was intelligent and very chatty. I was impulsive and maybe a little obnoxious, asking lots of questions. Later, I understood that this behavior was a mask protecting me from vulnerability.

Having witnessed physical abuse at age three, my Inner Supervillain came to believe that challenging the men in my life could have dire consequences. This belief probably kept me quiet as I became an abuse victim at age ten. For several years after that, if I spoke, it was probably a lie.

Who I really was inside was a mystery to everyone, but no more than me. I had no idea who I was.

I went on to spend decades pleasing, performing, and perfecting my way through life, always trying to prove myself as capable, strong, and reliable. I had gotten my first job at fourteen and never stopped working. Even when I had my kids, I had a side hustle going. Back at work, I succeeded, mainly because the parameters were clear, and I was driven and determined to prove my value.

As a journalist, I was fiercely competitive, quickly rising to win awards in college, and then landed a job at a dying paper in Santa Monica, CA.

Unfortunately, I hated it. When I returned to school for my bachelor's, I brought the same verve. I remember feeling such confidence in my ability to learn and write.

However, my personal relationships were a mess. The lines were constantly changing; I'd inevitably choose the 'least right' person for me. I felt like I had a sign on my back saying, "Hey, wrong guy! Pick me!"

And that is one of the reasons I stayed in that marriage for 13 years. It was almost as if I had a dual life. At work, I had confidence and aptitude that led some of my colleagues to make their way to my desk and jealously tell me I seemed to have the most fantastic life. They'd congratulate mo on my organization and prowess. It seemed to them that I also had the perfect husband–a millionaire taking me to travel several times per year.

But there was so much that no one knew. It wasn't just my husband wearing the mask, either. I hid it all behind my deep desire to prove myself and have the acceptance of others. People treating me like I was a millionaire was pretty awesome. Or so I thought at the time. Later, I would come to realize that none of my friendships were real. By then, I had been completely isolated from my family.

Again, I share all this with you, not to write my memoir but to show you how the programming weaves together.

By age 40, I was learning that I could do some fantastic things away from my husband. But in his presence, I was a bit of a mouse. I remember one conversation in particular that changed my life.

A couple we used to spend a lot of time with lived just 40 minutes away, and one time, the wife, Sam, invited me up to do some shopping and then hang out at her pool. We had a terrific day; we shopped and shared stories, and that evening at her pool over wine, she looked at me in shock and said, "You're so much fun–I had no idea."

I was taken aback by her statement. "I've always been me," I ventured, "How do I seem different?"

She explained that when my husband was around, I hardly spoke and was pretty reserved or short when I did. If you knew me better, you would see how crazy that sounds. I am in no way quiet or reserved.

That comment sent me back into therapy. And finally, I found a therapist who helped me see I needed to escape that abusive marriage. It was the very beginning of truly finding my voice. I was 43 years young.

In an excellent article I read on NeuroLeadership in 2020, writer Chris Weller states, "Finding your voice is an essential step towards unlocking your true potential. Your insights and ideas deserve to be heard, and when you speak up, you empower yourself to shape your own narrative."

Your voice can be a reflection of your inner strength, and it can transform not only your life but also the lives of those around you. That is not to say that there is anything wrong or less substantial in those who choose to be quiet and reflective. But allowing others to silence us or make us smaller stunts our growth. It took me a long time, but I learned on this journey of self-discovery and empowerment that our past does not have to dictate our present or future. We each have the ability to rewrite our story, one courageous word at a time.

In a world that has often assigned women secondary roles, learning not to make ourselves smaller for others can be an act of revolution. Throughout history, we've been squeezed into molds that don't fit our true potential, forced to shrink ourselves to work within the confines of our culturescape's daunting expectations. But change is possible, and when we lift each other up, we can start to see that our voices are catalysts for transformation and empowerment.

The power of speaking up for oneself dismantles the archaic notion that our role is merely to be seen and not heard. For some of us, this is a silly construct to even mention in 2023. But I have had several clients who, due to their culturescape, carry the remnants of that tired, old belief. And so, when a woman raises her voice, she defies these age-old stereotypes and declares that her thoughts, experiences, and viewpoints are not only valid but vital to the conversation. When was the last time you thought before walking into a meeting, "They need to hear what I have to say because it is vital"?

At the heart of this new belief is the rejection of the idea that women should be submissive or apologetic about who we are. By making ourselves smaller, we don't deny our growth; we unwittingly endorse a system that stifles our brilliance. When we speak up, we reclaim the space we deserve and inspire others to follow suit.

Think about the last time you apologized. Was it today? Here is a fun one: Make hash marks on a sticky note every time you apologize for a week.

The significance of women's voices extends far beyond our personal empowerment. We inject diversity into the discourse when we share our stories and opinions. Our myriad of voices enrich conversations, challenge the status quo, and ignite fresh, innovative ideas. And we need those!

Speaking up for oneself also serves as a beacon of courage and self-respect, showing the world that we value ourselves and our contributions. In a world that often tries to sideline us, asserting our worth becomes an assertion of our humanity.

But let's be real; speaking up isn't always a walk in the park, especially when societal norms have ingrained doubt into our minds. The fear of backlash or criticism can be paralyzing. This is why creating safe spaces where women can speak freely is paramount. Supporting one another in this endeavor establishes a network of solidarity that encourages us to break through the barriers designed to keep us small.

In our journey to reclaim our voice, doing so with authenticity is paramount. Demonstrating that perfection is not a hard requirement for discourse is an excellent way to show the next generation that we want to hear what they say and that they have value.

If I told you how long I waited to write this book, as I waited for some magic level of perfection before I dared to put myself out there, you would agree that with as much as I have to share, waiting is tantamount to silent submission.

All that said, I must acknowledge that speaking up can be daunting, especially when we've been conditioned to second-guess ourselves or, worse, doubt our worth. The dread of facing backlash or violence can be all too real.

This is where creating nurturing environments for authentic discourse becomes crucial. Uplifting each other in this journey for self-expression empowers us, and this transformation isn't just about us individually; it's about reshaping the world towards equality and inclusivity.

Okay. I'll put my soapbox away now and tell you about Maude.

Maude is a former client with a story that resonated deeply with me. She came to me after years of feeling unheard and invisible in her workplace. She was exceptionally talented, with a mind full of innovative ideas, but she often found herself stifled by self-doubt and a fear of speaking up. Being an expert in aerospace engineering, this incredible woman is a glass ceiling smasher and a ground-breaker.

However, in our sessions, Maude shared how her early experiences had molded her into a silent observer. She had grown up in a household where her opinions were rarely valued, and any attempts to assert herself were met with dismissal.

This pattern continued as she navigated her career in a male-dominated industry, leaving her with a nagging feeling that anything she thought to contribute was inconsequential.

Her work with her Inner Supervillain revealed many beliefs she had internalized. In time, she realized that her silence was not a sign of her weakness but had become a coping mechanism she had developed to protect herself from the potential backlash of speaking up.

Slowly, Maude started to experiment with using her voice. She joined an art and wine group and practiced expressing her ideas in this safe, mostly female space. Yes, a little wine helped!

But seriously, as Maude navigated her safe space, not only did she receive positive feedback, she blew them away with her brilliance. Her new friends wanted to learn more about the incredible projects she worked on and the robot she had invented. Her confidence blossomed, and she discovered her place as a brilliant mind.

Later, Maude also learned how to reframe her past experiences, recognizing that her worth was not determined by others' reactions. Even without her new group of friends, she understood that she had value and that regardless of what others thought or said, she had earned her own respect, which was invaluable.

Around that time, an opportunity arose at her workplace for employees to contribute ideas for a new project. Maude decided to seize the moment. She prepared her thoughts, organized her points, and pitched her idea with conviction. To her surprise, her colleagues were both receptive and genuinely impressed by her insights.

This experience marked a turning point for Maude. She discovered that her voice held power, and her perspective was valuable. As she continued to practice speaking up, her contributions became increasingly integral to her team's success.

As we continued to work together, Maude went through the usual ups and downs of personal growth. Her father passed, which led to many challenges, where old core beliefs surfaced, and she had to revisit work she thought was behind her. "Why the hell does this happen?" she said, leaning forward toward the camera in Zoom.

"It is all part of the fun journey of self-discovery," I replied sarcastically.

What Maude really wanted to know is a question I receive from almost every client at some point, particularly now that I usually only take on clients willing to work for a year–and Maude's situation is a perfect example of why I adjusted my contract.

Coaching can be a lot like scaling a challenging mountain. It comes with its share of victories and setbacks. Because life is a series of peaks and valleys, the deep inner work involved reflects that. Having a coach is like having a climbing guide, but our internal compass ensures we go in the right direction.

A coach is there to provide insight, offer tools, cheer, challenge, and deeply listen. As much as we'd like them to, a coach can not (and should not) provide the map. We must determine our own way.

Just like on the rugged terrain, we sometimes stumble, slip, and even fall–but that's where the magic of the journey lies.

When we falter and tumble, it is not a defeat. It is a chance to rise stronger, wiser, and more innovative. Sure, it hurts. And not just our bum. It can also damage our pride and even make us want to quit. But, just as a climber doesn't give up after a fall, we, too, must dust ourselves off and keep going.

Here's what is cool about having a coach: When we do fall (and we will fall), our coach is right there, ready to listen, ask compelling questions, and challenge us to get going again. Each setback teaches us resilience, fuels our determination, and strengthens our resolve. And as we ascend, the view becomes more breathtaking with every step forward.

Every fall teaches us where to find our footing and remember the actions that provide stability. We recognize strategies and insights that propel us forward. With experience under our belts, we can approach challenges with a wiser perspective and an arsenal of tools to tackle them head-on.

Working with a coach and doing this work isn't about avoiding falls; it's about navigating them with grace. I said as much to Maude that day.

She knew I was right, but that didn't help her to like it. Look: None of us do. As I work with my incredible coach, those days arrive where I winge because here I am, dirt on my face, on the ground. Lessons learned? Indeed–but I'm rarely happy about it.

The path may be challenging, but the view from the top is worth every stumble along the way.

How are you doing with voice? Are you avoiding any circumstances or situations that require you to speak up?

Homework

Here's a bit of homework for you:

Spend some time finding a safe space to challenge yourself to use your voice more.

When I was looking for that space, I joined Toastmasters. It was fun, but I prefer Maude's idea of joining a wine group.

The weight of silence can feel profound, a burden to shoulder. However, embracing one's voice becomes a practice of being authentic while establishing an environment for growth and incredible transformation.

Maude made it to the top of her mountain and is regarded as an expert voice in her field.

In a time craving change, femme leaders must forge a future where our contributions are celebrated, our narratives are cherished, and our influence is undeniable. The moment is ripe for women to stand tall, speak up unwaveringly, and seize our space–and the echoes of our voices will resound for generations to come.

— SIX —

Boundaries
Characters & Sacred Boundaries

Oh, do I ever have a lot to say about boundaries! It is time to break out my analogies again. This topic is one of my favorites because while we all know that we need boundaries, very few of us actually set them. Even fewer of us enforce them.

Before we get into setting boundaries, I frame the various characters using mythology to describe these characters to allow us to 'play' with these characters in our imagination. I will start with the challenging ones:

SHAPESHIFTERS

They are no joke. For those of us who have been in seriously toxic relationships—whether romantic, friendships, or even work relationships, we know that Shapeshifters can be truly insidious and cunning. They can change their face on a flip of a coin.

They are usually very charming and often intense.

They come with a game plan and know how to execute it well. That is why even a little awareness can go a long way.

So, how do we recognize Shapeshifters if they're constantly changing form?

What can we do to be more aware of them and the powers they wield? And how do we protect our sacred spaces?

Let's start with the red flags of a Shapeshifter.

While these aren't the only red flags, they are indeed the clearest and often followed in a shockingly precise order.

Shapeshifters infiltrate our lives. We can quickly get drawn in because this face is so interested in learning everything about us. After all, who doesn't love it when someone leans in, paying a lot of attention to what we say and care about?

Behind the scenes, though, they are using this information to make themselves indispensable and, later, to do the most damage. Initially, though, they do their best to impress us with generosity or grandiose acts of kindness. They seem remarkably intuitive, knowing precisely what we want and need. It will seem too good to be true–because it is.

On a chartered plane, nibbling strawberries and drinking champagne, the focused company of a Shapeshifter can be intoxicating.

As they get to know what makes us tick, they can get conspiratory–pitting two against the world.

However, this friendly, "there is only us" face is merely designed to pre-pare us for the next stage: Isolation. For some, it's chirping in our ear about our best friends or relatives. For others, the face quickly shifts to become one of explosive jealousy, wild accusations, or other toxic behaviors.

HOW YOU KNOW

⚐ Infilitrate your life

⚐ Make themselves indispensable

⚐ Often seem too good to be true (for a while)

⚐ Conspiratory (the two of you against the world)

⚑ Begin isolating you by complaining about or instigating conflicts with those you are close to and may potentially see through them

⚑ Lots of toxic behaviors such as gaslighting, demeaning, bullying, blaming, exploiting, etc.

Shapeshifters can actually be anyone. The idea that they can only be the men we love just isn't accurate. These characters easily shift into the role of friends, relatives, co-workers, or employees.

Let's establish a genuine truth: Shapeshifters are not people we can fix. Nor should we try.

Remembering those red flags can save you a lot of time. I call these characters Shapeshifters because they tend to come back–over and over again, even if it's in the form of a different human. You will want to get skilled at noticing those red flags. As a Shapeshifter expert, I have to be honest here and tell you that the best action you can take when you recognize one–is to run.

ENERGY VAMPIRES

While their energy can be draining and even toxic, I don't actually fear them. Why? Because we can create boundaries for energy vampires.

I do not mean to suggest that it's easy. Energy Vampires can also be anyone–romantic partners, friends, family, co-workers, and so on. If you find that you are particularly sensitive to these characters, perhaps an empath, you will want to take additional steps to protect yourself. We'll circle back to that at the end of this chapter.

In the meantime, let's look at a few of the traits of the Energy Vampire.

These characters bring a heavy energy into the room. If you are particularly sensitive, it can feel physical. You may feel your energy being zapped or drained, and sometimes, you might feel their heavy energy stick around even after they've gone.

They tend to be on the negative side, but this isn't always true. Needing to feast on your attention and empathy, they might always have some drama going on. If so, it is pervasive. They always have a story to tell you where *they* are the victim.

Because they are draining and bring this energy into your spaces or 'fill up the room' with their neediness, feeling dread about being in their company isn't surprising, even if they are family or a close friend.

Gaslighting is very common with energy vampires because, after all– nothing is their fault.

HOW YOU KNOW

⚐ You can feel their 'heavy' energy when they walk into the room

⚐ You feel zapped or drained from being in their presence

⚐ You might think of them as being negative or a real downer

⚐ You find yourself dreading their company

⚐ Conflict with them can end up with you being cast as the bad guy

If you are making a connection to the behaviors of a narcissist or Shapeshifter here, sure. But upon closer examination, it's only a couple of boxes you'd be ticking–so let's not get into diagnosing unhealthy or even toxic behaviors as a bona fide personality disorder.

However, if you see many red flags, that is more concerning, and this individual may not be a mere energy vampire.

Additional characters I'll mention in passing are:

The Drama Royalty–who always focus on themselves and some personal or professional drama.

The Meanie–who spends a lot of their time talking shit behind, well, everyone's backs.

Protection from these particular characters is more complicated because they come with the environment. You'll want to keep them at arm's length if possible. And that can be a challenge. That brings us to family.

A brief note on family:

Family is often where we find the dream-stealer. This character simply points out why whatever dream we share will undoubtedly go bust.

This dream-stealing behavior doesn't always have to be nefarious. This family member may be responding to their own trauma, programmed core beliefs, or it could simply be their energetic level on that particular day.

Family members who feel a little, or even a lot, draining energetically and those who we consider truly toxic can definitely pose a challenge for us. With family, there are different and longer-lasting consequences when we try to set boundaries with them.

Due to the highly complicated nature of family relationships, we have to weigh our discomfort with whatever that consequence may be. Keep this in mind as we get into setting boundaries.

I know you have been categorizing the characters in your life mentally, but here is a brief exercise for you: Grab a sheet of paper that you can burn or throw away later and categorize the people in your life. You will find the task eye-opening, which will help you as we do some boundary placement in just a bit here.

We have just one more character type to discuss.

ENERGETIC BLESSINGS

For apparent reasons, this is my favorite character to have around. Let's jump right into how you know you are in the presence of an Energetic Blessing:

✓ We feel drawn to Energetic Blessings because they have a high vibration level. There is no drama.

✓ We tend to want to aim higher when they are around us because they bring positive energy.

✓ They aren't afraid to call us out on our bullshit and honestly want us to be happy. When we get in our own way, they are the first to mention it.

✓ Because they come from a place of love, they don't let our dark moments bother them. They approach us with empathy and are even willing to join us in our pity party when needed. Afterward, they are there to pull us off the couch and kick us in the ass.

✓ Honestly, it's just fun to be around them–but in a healthy way. They make us want to be healthier and raise our energy level. That's why we call them blessings.

If you're a fan of Bridesmaids, remember Melissa McCarthy's character Megan? She goes to Annie's (Kristen Wig) house, literally gets on top of her, and kicks her ass off the couch–giving her friend a wake-up call. She is an Energetic blessing.

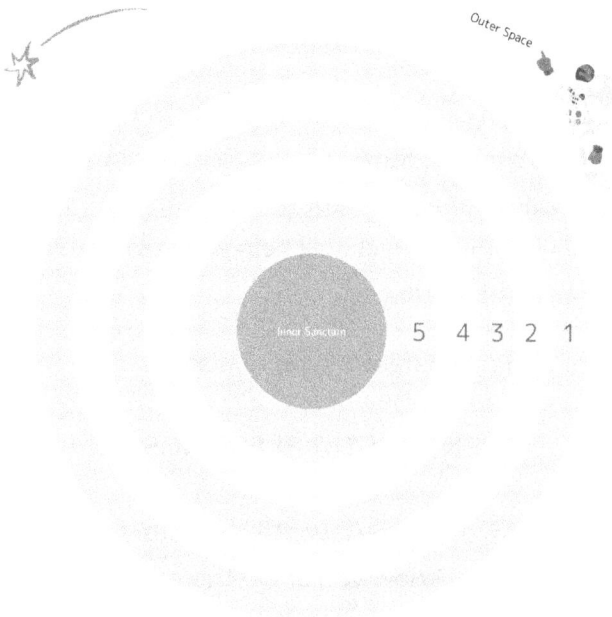

Outer Space

Inner Sanctum   5   4   3   2   1

SETTING BOUNDARIES

Ready to start assigning some boundaries? You know the characters in your life. It is time to begin with the basics of zone assignment. In the chart below, you can pencil in some names or categories of characters. Be prepared to move them around as needed.

I'll begin with an example of how I use this simple diagram to do my zone assignment:

My Inner Sanctum is just for me. No one else is allowed into that space. This is the space for dreams, goals, and purpose. It is a space to connect our higher self and our Inner Supervillain.

Zone Five is for the person I share my most intimate shame shitstorm with. When I've said or done something I wouldn't confess to anyone else, this is who I call. For me, this person is my coach.

Zone Four is where my best friend hangs out. She is an energetic blessing. And while that is true, there are some things about myself I hold back a bit that I might share only with my coach. This zone might work well for a spouse or partner as well.

When I think about these two zones, I consider trust and the limits of what I am willing to share. Brené Brown says it best when she asserts, "They should have to earn your story."

Zone Three is usually for a whole bunch of people. I share much less with them. I ask myself, "Have they earned it?"

Invariably, the answer is 'no' or 'not yet.' Here is a tip: Dream-stealers are not allowed anywhere near my Zone Three, period. There is still a level of trust in this Zone, and I have learned not to trust a Dream-stealer with my personal stories, even if they are family.

That said, please design any rules that apply to you based on your preference.

Zone Two is for my distant relationships, where we don't speak intimately or frequently. This zone may also be certain colleagues or family members.

Zone One is what I call my 'Last Chance' zone. This is where I place people who have hurt me or broken my trust. I put them here before I release them into the last zone. This zone is also for acquaintances and general colleagues.

And then we have Outer Space. This is where I put people I am unwilling to entirely remove from my life, either because I've decided it is too complicated or because the consequences are not worth it to me. Energy Vampires tend to hang out here.

Okay! Congratulations! You have just completed the easy part of setting your boundaries.

The next step is to take some notes on your zones. What is and what is not allowed? What does a breach look like? When is it time to move someone to another zone?

The thing with boundaries is that some characters can sense they've been moved into another zone and don't like their new assignment. Others don't like limitations at all, particularly if there haven't been any boundaries in place for them up to this point.

The downright childish temper tantrums and other immature behaviors could come as a surprise. So let's briefly prepare.

First comes your voice, which is why we covered that before. You will need to speak up and establish the boundary. The trickiest part for my clients is figuring out what they want to say, so I recommend preparing a short list of comfortable statements.

Let's Play with this! Say I am having a little party, and my mom calls, saying she plans on bringing her dog. There will be several clients there, and she knows this. Additionally, her dog peed on my carpet the last time he was over. My gut response is to get angry at how rude it is to assume rather than ask. Now that I'm already annoyed, I want to say, are you kidding me?

Or, because I am annoyed, I might want to say nothing at all to avoid a confrontation or fight. But characters in Zone Three haven't earned the right to make assumptions about my personal space, nor what they bring into my sanctuary, which is my home. I need to speak up for myself and my boundaries in a calm, reasoned way.

First, I can say, "Mom, I'd love to have you, but I'm uncomfortable with you bringing your dog to the party. I would like you to please leave the dog at home."

The part of boundaries that no one likes to talk about is what the consequences will be for a breach, and what about the consequences we might have to accept for laying down the law?

Playing this scenario out in my head, I realize my mom also has choices.

Response #1 could be, "Fine, then I'll stay home."

And my reply is then, "Well, I'd love to have you, but that's certainly your choice. I understand."

This is me accepting a possible outcome. I have already predetermined that I am okay with this option.

Response #2 could be, "Why? He won't bother you? What's the big deal?"

Here, the energy shifts, and I begin to feel drained. It is awkward, and depending on my reply, we can easily have a conflict. I choose not to explain. I make a statement.

"Mom, please respect my boundary here. Again, I'd love to have you, but the dog needs to stay at home."

Response #3 could be agreement.

Response #4 could be that she is angry, hangs up the phone, and doesn't attend my party.

Response #5 could be that she shows up with the damn dog.

It gets tricky here, doesn't it? We have a history. She knows I'd rather not have a confrontation. She can easily take advantage of that history.

The bottom line is how important my party is to me, or as the old saying goes, I've got to choose my battles wisely.

Depending on the character we are interacting with, the ensuing 'battle' may not be worth it. That is why we should practice! We know the characters in our lives pretty well, don't we? As a result, we are pretty good at guessing how they might respond.

Here are some handy sentence starters that may be helpful:

In this situation, what I need is...

I'd love to have you, but I'm not comfortable with...

In the future, I'd like to set the boundary that...

I need to tell you that I'm not okay with...

What I prefer is...

And then there is my favorite. No.

In my workshops, I love to work with a group of driven women who also struggle with the simple response of "No."

Why do we always have to pad the no with a bunch of reasoning? Why do we feel we need to add the because followed by a bunch of BS explanations?

We don't want to, right? So then, why do we?

Why not just say a simple no and leave it hanging in the air?

I'll confess there are probably times we want to add a touch of gentle kindness or polite rebuttal, but do we need to do that every time? No.

What I hear most often from clients is that they dread having to say no because they (pleasing) don't want to disappoint anyone or (performing) want to ensure someone's respect or acceptance or (perfecting) never, ever want to get it wrong.

Let's play with this! Practice saying no. Here are a half-dozen ways to get you started:

No.
It's kind of you to ask, but no.
No, thank you.
I've given it some thought and have decided no.
Not this time; perhaps another time.
It's tempting, but I'm going to say no.

My daughter and I love this one:
I am disinclined to acquiesce to your request.

As promised, I would like to chat about various ways to protect your energy, especially if you are sensitive.

I will get a little science meets Spirit here, and some of what I say may feel a bit woo. But as a psychology and neuroscience nerd, I'll keep one foot on the ground for you.

In the quantum field, all things are possible. With God, Universe, Source, Goddess, Collective—in us, as us, all things are possible.

From my extensive research and experience, here is the secret behind the secret:

Creation is part of our gifts, whether we've had children or not. We still get it. We have a knowing. But let's go deeper. Energy is real. It is around us and within us all of the time. We project and reflect energy as well as consume it.

Suppose we take back our power by refusing to allow other's expectations, disappointments, and frustrations into our space? We can vibrate at a much higher frequency if we get connected to the spirit side of our being. We can access the quantum field. We can create. We can master ourselves. I invite you to consider this, and continue to be open to insight as you complete this book.

Sage is a great way to cleanse and protect your home space.

Bundles can be purchased at local shops and farmer's markets, as well as Amazon. There are tons available. I'm particularly partial to bundles from

Mama Wunderbar on Amazon because I like their vibe and the various options.

I just go through my home with my smoking sage and a big feather I found. I repeat a phrase that just came to me one day, and it's always served me well. I simply say, "Only energy of light and love are permitted to enter this house." I make sure I get every corner and all the doors and windows. Then, I use sand in an abalone shell to put it out.

How often this is done is your choice. I usually get to it every month or so and sage my office area before every client to ensure I bring my best energy.

Crystals are a great way to vibe up your home or immediate space and amplify your energy. Also, they make a great little protection zone. Our ancestors have valued crystals for ages, and humans have used stones for healing and energy work for thousands of years. I've got a fine collection in my home and use them regularly.

Can I provide scientific proof of what they can do? Nope. I can explain how quartz, in particular, can hold 360 terabytes of information. I can tell you that the ancient Egyptians, Chinese, Greeks, and Romans all used crystals for medicine, healing, and protection.

I can also tell you about the placebo effect, which any decent article found in a Google result will certainly do. But honestly, for me—they just work.

I cleanse my crystals in water or by smudging them with sage. It is also popular to cleanse with sunlight or moonlight. I have also made a spray of witch hazel, sage, and cedarwood essential oils for water-safe crystals (crystals that end in ite tend not to be water-safe).

Here is a method I use to charge my favorite crystals (quartz and amethyst) that was taught to me by a world-renowned psychic medium:

I play soothing spiritual music or shamanic drums, depending on my mood, and get into a meditative state by closing my eyes and breathing deeply.

I hold my crystal in my left palm and cover it with my right.

As I relax, I imagine a pure white light pouring from the Universe into the top of my head and see it rush through my body, swirling pure, positive, healing light through my entire body.

I then hold the crystal to my heart and imagine the light pausing there to swirl and fill my heart with protective positivity. Then I imagine that light filling the crystal.

Voila! The crystal is charged and ready to protect me throughout the week.

Before I close this little meditation session, I push the white light out of my body to create a beautiful protective bubble around me. Then, I open my eyes.

I repeat this process each day with the collection of crystals I keep on my desk.

I promised I'd keep one foot on the ground, right? Psychologically and practically speaking, belief is literally everything.

Beyond belief, it is important to note that these little ceremonies, practiced regularly, train our subconscious to repel negativity and call in positivity. Our subconscious then looks for opportunities to keep our spaces free of other people's negative bullshit.

I'll call that a win/win and leave it at that.

With one foot still firmly planted on the ground, let's talk about meditation.

A meta-analysis including nearly 1,300 adults found that meditation can decrease anxiety. An eight-week study where participants practiced regular meditation reduced levels of the stress hormone cortisol.

One review of treatments given to more than 3,500 adults found that meditation improved symptoms of depression.

A study of 153 adults showed reduced feelings of loneliness and anxiety after practicing meditation, and that experience in meditation may cultivate problem-solving skills.

That's just the beginning.

Science-based benefits of meditation include the reduction of stress, management of the symptoms of anxiety, asthma, cancer, chronic pain, heart disease, depression, high blood pressure, and irritable bowel syndrome. It can also promote our emotional health, lengthen our attention span, enhance self-awareness, generate kindness, help us fight addictions and reduce age-related memory loss.

Boom.

If there is any one thing you could do for your health that would make the most significant impact, studies continue to show that meditation is it. Period.

Additionally, you connect with yourself and your superpowers. Your intuition dials in. Your energy vibrates at a much higher level, and because of this, meditation is an excellent tool for protecting yourself energetically.

I meditate twice daily. I complete a 20-minute shorty in the morning and a more extended 45-minute to an hour session at night. It took me a long time to make these habits stick. But practicing meditation has changed my life more than I can mention in this chapter.

I believe in meditation so much I ensure that I speak about it to every client multiple times. I also provide guided meditation recordings.

There are some incredible apps out there for meditation. Check out Soulvana, Calm, and Headspace. All are good, and I believe they each have a free version.

Here is where the rubber meets the road with this work: It is all about the habits here.

Creating boundaries does us no good at all if we don't ensure we express them. Nor do they serve us if we do not consistently and firmly manage them. If we fail to exercise our own personal rights with each of the characters in our lives, then as my mother so aptly said, because we teach them how to treat us, we can't be surprised by the results.

Remember these five rules above all:

- Honor your sacred boundaries.

- Make no excuses for your choices.

- Be kind and compassionate but firm.

- Ensure they have earned your stories.

- Forgive yourself when you break the first four rules and try again.

·

— SEVEN —

Having it All

Driven women struggle with the dilemma of trying to succeed in a culturescape that not only rewards stereotypical male values–but prefers them. This culturescape also demands that we simultaneously be attractive, desirable, and connected to our femininity.

Seeking achievement involves competitiveness, assertiveness, and confidence–traits that in women are instead labeled as aggressive, pushy, and conjure the image of a 'bitch with a briefcase.'

Women generally prefer using a more cooperative leadership style; however, more often than not, must navigate the expectations and rules for success that have been designed for men by men.

I think it essential to point out that many of us enjoy the pursuit of achievement. While the number of us who also *need* to work is staggering compared to just twenty years ago, we also *want* to climb the mountain of our mission, passion, and calling. And we *want* to reach the top. The problem is the top just isn't enough.

What success means to a woman is very different than what it means to a man. Men mostly see success as their work, income, and status. As driven women, we only *count* our success if it is all-encompassing, including our personal lives.

In short, we believe we need to "have it all" to consider ourselves successful.

To *have* it all, driven women feel they must *do* it all–by themselves, at a tremendous cost to their physical and emotional well-being.

Caught between our worlds, we are doomed to fail in one half of our life or the other. We must sacrifice either our personal relationships or ourselves and those we lead.

It is no wonder that women are twice as likely to experience work-related stress symptoms like ulcers, sleep issues, perception and memory disorders, anxiety or depression, chronic fatigue, cardiovascular disease, backache, headache, recurrent viral infections, and more.

These symptoms, of course, are just enough to disrupt–but not enough to diagnose–allowing us to continue the habit of pulling up our proverbial bootstraps and pushing through as more severe illnesses incubate.

Socially, however, we celebrate and admire the dazzling accomplishments of the woman who can keep her plates spinning while the rest of us pick up the broken pieces, feeling inadequate.

What we need to recognize is the truth that this celebrated, ideal woman is also trapped by the worthiness hustle. You see, the more she proves she can do, the higher the expectations rise. And with everyone watching, this paragon feels she must stretch her resources even thinner to maintain her standing, keep everyone happy, etc.

There is also a generational pressure at play. Fully aware that we bear the responsibility of *proving* we can *perform* within the upper stratum of professional power, we must then *perfect* the art and science of doing it all, spinning our plates on the high wire of other's expectations.

While all this is true, we still want more–for ourselves and for those who follow in our footsteps. We want to achieve more, earn more, and experience more. We are all at once driven, exhausted, and burdened with guilt and shame.

As driven women, we are rushed. We are almost always in a hurry, competitive, and preoccupied with how much or how many. We tend to do everything rapidly, rushing about as we move, talk, eat, and work, thinking and speaking in a rapid cadence, impatiently finishing other's sentences.

If any of these descriptors sound familiar, it is because they are just the surface behaviors of what

Meyer Friedman and Ray Rosenman deemed "Type A Personality" in the 1950s.

It is important to note that research from the University of Toronto published in the Journal of Personality and Social Psychology suggests that categorizing people's personalities into Type A, B, C, or D is an outdated practice.

Trends change, even in psychology; however, our subconscious thinks little about current trends and instead responds to what she sees, hears, tastes, smells, and touches. We, therefore, often repeat behavior patterns we have witnessed or experienced, regardless of the shifting sands of psychological research practices.

Let's talk about Ruth.

The pressure to do well in Ruth's family goes back several generations, but for her, encapsulated in the stories of her grandparents. Each survived unimaginable experiences in WWII Concentration camps and impressed upon their descendants the importance not only in succeeding but in making the world a better place for future generations.

Ruth's mother had been an editor for a large publishing house, and her father was a doctor. Her uncle is still a renowned rocket scientist. As a CEO, you'd think Ruth would feel she had made her grandparents proud; however, as she described it, she just couldn't seem to measure up.

Ruth had started as an assistant and later became a corporate trainer. Every two years or so, there was a new title before her name. Along the way, she sacrificed what seemed necessary. There were work relationships, personal relationships, and countless hours of sleep set aside to make way for her achievements. To put it mildly, her hustle was all-encompassing, her rise meteoric.

The year before being named CEO, the board chair contacted Ruth with the company survey results. The words used by the employees to characterize her leadership style were "cold, unfeeling, and short." She was told any promotion was tied to demonstrating improvement.

"Do you think a man would be asked to change these characteristics," Ruth demanded, "Would their promotion be on the line?"

Ruth was right. The likelihood of a man even being characterized this way was slim, let alone having a board chair approach him to alter it. But because it mattered to Ruth that her employees felt she was not demonstrating enough 'feelings' toward them, she launched a program called TEAM.

Her program afforded an opportunity for the employees to lead various workshops and sessions on topics such as wellness in the workplace, art, equity, culture, cooking, and more. That next year, Ruth was named CEO.

The following year, at age 43, Ruth finally had a child. Sam was her miracle baby. Concerned with demonstrating weakness, possibly being replaced, or revealing an inability to balance her work and personal life, she returned to the office part-time within six weeks.

Now, as she spoke to me a year later, the pressure of keeping it all going made Ruth feel as though her life was seriously beginning to unravel.

As she described her experience, Ruth spoke staccato-like, seeming impatient and stressed. When I started to ask a question, she would interrupt me, finish my question, and launch into a synopsis answer. Finally, she looked at me and said, "Tell me how to fix this."

Accustomed to calling her people into a room, describing a problem, and getting quick results, there was an expectation of my ability to provide an actionable, timely solution.

Of course, I could not deliver what Ruth wanted, and I told her so. There was no quick fix–no magic pill. Without hesitation, I told Ruth I had concerns about whether working with me would help her. For the first time in an hour, Ruth was still and silent. It was clear that she hadn't expected this outcome. I explained that based on her demeanor and clearly unrealistic expectations of what working with me would entail, I thought it possible that Ruth was not ready at that time.

Hot tears began to roll down Ruth's face. "I don't understand," she sniffed, "I thought you could help me like you helped Chris." Her back stiffened, "So this has all been a waste of time?"

There is little considered worse to a driven woman than wasting her time. I could see that Ruth felt betrayed. She thought she had been led to believe I could fix her right up so she could resume her busy life. With six-figure fees for a year of Elite, Bespoke Coaching, damn right, I'd better have a solution. I appreciated her point of view.

I think Ruth was stunned I would leave fees like that on the table–and possibly that my doing so meant she was a hopeless case. I could tell by her slumped shoulders she was feeling a bit defeated.

My concern was that Ruth did not appear ready to sign up for the deep introspection required when working with a coach. Even when her career advancement had been on the line, rather than focus on relationship building with her team, she had created a program where *her employees* revealed their passions and personal sides while *she* remained safe in her office, being no more vulnerable than she had been previously.

Additionally, her impatience at 'fixing' her life with what appeared to be an outside solution, while understandable, would not help her in any real way. And her answers to my unfinished questions were clearly prepared, indicating that her Inner

Supervillain had a "You shall not pass" sign firmly in place.

Ruth would need to be willing to work with her subconscious and build trust and rapport with me. There would be much more difficult questions if we worked together, and–she would need to be willing to sit with not having answers to some questions about her feelings, attitudes, and behaviors. She would have to be okay with uncertainty and vulnerability.

"And that is why we work together for a year," I concluded, "The journey is a bit like climbing a mountain. When you fall–and you will fall, having your coach at your side makes all the difference. But you have to be willing to risk falling and getting dirty along the way."

Having had my own coach for quite some time, I spoke from personal experience, not just from a coach's perspective.

When I began my coaching training, I remember reading something from a mentor. He asserted that as a coach, you must be willing to invest well beyond what is comfortable in coaching for yourself before ever establishing fees that make clients uncomfortable.

He is right–but it isn't just the contract amount we're discussing here. In my opinion, to be an exceptional coach, it is imperative to have been willing to invest your own time, trust, and deep introspection with another coach for at least one year before you can begin to ask it of a client.

For me, there was no risk involved in letting Ruth know I was concerned about her coachability because I had done and continue to do this work as a client with my own coach. I know exactly what it takes. If Ruth wasn't willing to seriously invest herself and risk challenging her habits, beliefs, and fears in this way, it would indeed be a waste of her time–and mine.

That said, I made sure to explain to Ruth that I was in no way trying to imply not being ready for this work made her inferior. Nor was I toying with her. Doing this deep inner work is no picnic, and one must go into it with eyes wide open, *very* much like climbing a mountain.

I told her I would hold the spot so she could take a week to think it over and then let me know.

One year later, Ruth started her own baby clothing company and pioneered a workplace environment with an in-the-building childcare center and two-hour breaks in the workday to allow for play and visitation. She proved that having more ready access to see our children throughout the day increases our productivity—even with the two one-hour breaks in the workday.

More importantly, the employees who benefited from these policies were *both* women and men.

To be clear, this genius had nothing to do with me. In working with me, Ruth simply learned to get out of her own way, where her genius was patiently waiting for release.

Ruth and I still talk once or twice per year. The challenge to find balance hasn't gone away, nor has the culturescape that perpetuates it. But she is now very clear on her values and priorities and knows which projects are an automatic hell-yes. Those that aren't, go into the 'never gonna happen' bin without guilt, shame, or concern of being less than.

74.7% of prime-age women (23-54) are working as of January 2023, according to the Bureau of Labor Statistics under the U.S. Department of Labor.

Unfortunately, the pay gap is still relatively high, with prime-age women earning 16 percent less than men. The pay gap is larger still among those aged 55–64, with women making 22 percent less than men at the median.

Additionally, women are 5 to 8 times more likely than men to have their employment affected by caregiver responsibilities.

Our concerns about balance will not disappear anytime soon, and Driven Woman Syndrome is a *cognitive-behavioral* syndrome. To really change our stress problems, we must change how we think, believe, and behave.

Frankly, our subconscious autopilots us through our day, and to make any lasting changes, we need to take an honest look at our culturescape *and* conduct an honest self-assessment. Only then will we be able to design new, healthier attitudes, beliefs, and habits that interrupt our vicious cycle of stress.

Stress is a social construct that is our very human way of adapting to our culturescape. In America specifically, we have adapted to a high-pressure, highly competitive, fast-paced work environment.

It is entirely fair to say that men have needed to adapt and have suffered the consequences of work-related stress; however, women have had to adapt to the rate of change, increased levels of multi-tasking, *and* are held up for inspection against a vastly different set of social and cultural norms.

Many of these women adapt to the increased demands by pushing themselves to *do* it all so they can demonstrate to the world that they can indeed *have* it all. Unfortunately, it can come at a significant cost to overall well-being.

As women, or those that identify as such, we appear to have arrived at a place where we need to lift each other up and support each other to ditch the worthiness hustle in favor of a more *designed* lifestyle.

— EIGHT —

Allowing

For a year or so, I did a podcast called Wild Femmepreneurs. Frustrated with the bullshit sales tactics I saw in my feed, I decided there should be a show highlighting femme founders. We would have real conversations about the challenges and blessings of being an entrepreneur. Some of the discussions were quite powerful.

I had already written my thesis on Driven Woman Syndrome. However, in doing this show, I was able to cultivate thirty-five more first-hand accounts that reveal all driven women have the same issues, regardless of our job title, race, or income.

One of the many challenges discussed repeatedly is this idea of allowing. I noticed that there is often a misunderstanding about what allowing looks like. Some women imagine it is sitting cross-legged chanting OM– waiting for all to arrive, be well, or get sorted. Others seem to think it a weak excuse not to act at all.

As I define it, allowing is accepting some things do not need our interference or manipulation. There are certain things that are not meant to be or will work out better if we just stay the hell out of it.

Sometimes, people need to learn for themselves. Other times, we must go through something to find our path to another. And on occasion, it will completely suck, hurt, or otherwise not turn out how we would like it to. I call it Outcome Disillusion when our magic formula of being in control doesn't go our way.

Driven women want control. Often, there is a trauma event somewhere, and we have collected stories around the idea that things just turn out better if we are the boss of them. I used to imagine a problem as a child, saying, "You're not the boss of me!"

My response was, "Wanna make a bet?"

I became so adept at solving challenging issues that I begged to take them on. I took pride in getting on the phone and changing the outcome to go in my favor. At work, colleagues would bring these special cases to my desk, knowing I would have the answer or be willing to take it on myself.

To this day, if I am overcharged or have an issue with the cable company or whatever, I know that if I am willing to suffer some time and patience speaking to several people, possibly repeating myself, and talking to supervisors, I can resolve the issue. Yay me!

I now weigh my options and decide if the outcome is worth investing that time and effort. I also choose to reserve this skill for my own particular use. No longer do I chomp at the bit for someone to invite me into their arena to do battle on their behalf.

Of course, trying to control or force is not the same as determination. Having a goal in mind, making the necessary preparations, and having the patience to see that it comes together is a good thing. Sometimes, it works out, and other times, it does not. So, we learn, pivot, and try a new approach or idea.

Then, there is control: Stubbornly trying to force something or someone to be what we want rather than what is. This exercise only makes us more frustrated, with potentially dire consequences.

Monique is a former client of mine who always made the deal happen. As the owner of a successful event management company in Las Vegas, Nevada, she knew how to make the magic happen. Managing the push and pull of what the client wanted versus what the event locations and her team could pull off was what she did best.

I met Monique when she was preparing to take her business to the next level, and she wanted a coach who could work with her to chase the impossible goal. She knew she was holding herself back, and having a coach might just make the difference.

Back then, I was doing workshops on building confidence castles, and Monique approached me afterward to chat about me becoming her coach.

"I know I need to work on being more confident in delivering client proposals," she explained, "and today was amazing, but I need more support."

When Monique and I met a couple of weeks later, she insisted that three months of working together would be plenty, and to my chagrin, I agreed. At the time, I was willing to put together 90-day contracts for intensive coaching.

As I worked with Monique, we spoke a lot about control, and the many occasions when trying to force the client relationship had burned a bridge.

In certain circumstances, Monique couldn't trust that her reputation and pitch were enough. She couldn't seem to allow the client to sit with her proposal and make the decision. She'd call and email to the point of harassment, often insisting they respond within 24 hours. After several sessions, Monique recognized this behavior was holding her back.

She practiced several scenarios where she would allow the client to make the decision, how it might feel to close the deal, and how she would pivot and recover when it did not go as planned. Monique had also begun to do the deep inner work related to why she felt the need to force the client into a contract with such intensity. She was starting to make real progress. And then, as it often goes around the three or four-month mark, something happened just a few weeks after our last session.

A considerable opportunity had presented itself. An A-list client wanted a stack of unreasonable perks and services. Monique wasn't prepared but considered how this client's business could open other doors for her. She put together the contract and worked behind the scenes to force her vendors to meet the A-lister's requests.

Multiple times, the deal looked like it just wouldn't happen. Some of the vendors weren't happy with the proposed timeline or the client's excessive demands. But, feeling desperate to make the deal happen, Monique made promises and took risks by paying advance bonuses to the vendors. She even promised the client an out-clause to get the deal done.

Monique was in a classic backslide. Remember how I said doing deep inner work is like mountain climbing? Yep. She fell hard. The client backed out of the contract, and tens of thousands were lost.

Initially, Monique was so distraught she blamed her coach. This work should have been successful in preventing her from making such a stupid mistake!

Fortunately, Monique later remembered that I had told her that back-sliding happens–we default to autopilot when intense emotions are at play. It takes practice to get beyond the trigger so we can instead observe and allow. Her choice to push the deal and take risks is exactly what she had been doing for years. Because it worked so many times in building her business, her subconscious had collected enough evidence that the gamble seemed worthwhile.

Outside of her urgent, rushed need to please, perform, and perfect her way into this contract, Monique could clearly see how her choices were precisely like standing in front of a slot machine.

This is not to say that risks in business are wrong; they aren't. We entrepreneurs make them all the time. But the bet of an out-clause was far too risky with all that was in play, and Monique knew it.

After a few weeks, Monique set an appointment with me. We spent another eight months working together after that, and today, her business is booming.

There was another allowing at play here. Monique also learned how to allow herself to grow and develop over time. Imagining that she could be completely confident and change years of habits in just three months wasn't fair. And feeling like she had to prove that she could reach this new level had been part of the undue pressure.

How do we learn this type of allowing when we are so entrenched in our hustle habits?

Three words. Change our expectations.

Let's roll back to how we *interpret* events in our lives. Imagine a morning when you wake up with a slight headache. As you grab your top, you notice the dry cleaner missed that stain you pointed out last week. You mumble something about how it figures as you work out another outfit and go to pour a cuppa before you dash out the door. You spill some coffee on the counter and a little splashes on your top. "Son of a…" you exclaim.

After a quick change and a murmur of how this is not your day, you get in your car and make your way to work. Three blocks down, you approach a four-way stop; however, the driver to your right continues right on through without stopping.

In split-second timing, you slam your foot on the break and safely stop without incident. The other driver appears unaffected, and off she goes.

"You shitty freaking driver," you yell after her, "You almost killed me!"

Your adrenaline is pumping, and the fight/flight response has kicked in. You are experiencing 'amygdala hijack.' The story your subconscious is weaving is all about how you almost died, so your body continues to respond accordingly. To make matters worse, you already interpreted your morning as not being your day.

The other driver, however, hums a happy tune as she makes her way to her destination, clearly interpreting the incident differently than you.

Our Inner Supervillain, aka our subconscious, reacts using perception, meaning-making, and expectation, or what I call the PME Cycle, to arrive at a response.

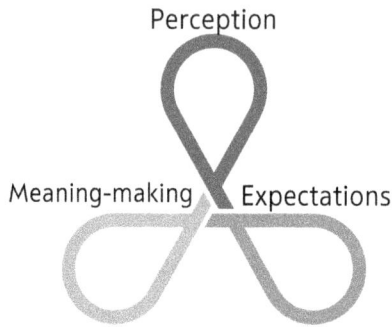

Perception

Meaning-making   Expectations

There's an assessment of well-being. Is there a threat to our security, values, or self-esteem?

Next, she sets about meaning-making. She asks important questions about what it means, what actions are necessary, etc.

The answers to these questions are based on our expectations created via the filters of our values, beliefs, assumptions, and internal stories about past experiences.

And then we respond with our state. This repeats, with each part of the cycle informing the other, leading to assumptions that can become distorted thinking, which is perceived as a threat to our security, values, or self-esteem, and on it goes.

How did the PME cycle affect Monique's decision to take a costly risk in her business? Let's look at that.

Monique perceived a threat to her new-found confidence when faced with the challenge of landing an A-list client.

The meaning-making was the question, "Am I good enough?" or perhaps, "How can I prove I am good enough?"

The expectation is often complicated, packed with layered beliefs, stories, and inaccurate evidence collected during our lifetime. For Monique, the expectation to prove she was good enough to land this client was simple. She was a single mother, and her father regularly said he thought her career choice was incredibly irresponsible.

Monique had been pushing herself hard to make a good life for her daughter and was willing to take the additional risk to prove her father wrong and show that she was a good provider and mother.

The distorted thinking became an 'all-or-nothing' statement that went something like, "If I don't close this deal and level up my business, I am proving that I am not good enough."

The expectation was, "I have to prove myself to everyone."

There are loads of these expectations that feed Driven Woman Syndrome. Here are just six.

- I have to please others by saying yes to their requests.

- I should be able to perform according to their expectations.

- I have to do things perfectly.

- Having it all should make me happy.

- I can't relax! There is too much to do!

- If I take care of everyone, I will be valued.

Working to change our expectations requires a serious commitment to befriending our Inner Supervillain. After all, she is the one running the PME Cycle on autopilot.

Here is an exercise to challenge her expectations. Use the six above, or write down any additional expectations you may have noticed. Ask her *why* this is true and keep challenging until she runs out of gas.

Example:

I have to please others by saying yes to their requests.

Why?

Because if I say no, there will be consequences.

What consequences?

They won't like me.

Why does this matter?

Because I have to be liked to be happy.

Why?

Because it hurts when people are mean.

And there it is. When we arrive at answers like this, it is an excellent time to stop. We know there is an incident (or several) behind a statement like that; we need not dig deeper. Just the awareness that this expectation comes from generalizations and exaggerated thinking can help us reframe the entire PME cycle. With consistent practice, the autopilot can become more grounded.

Monique's work to challenge her expectation that "I have to prove myself to everyone" was distilled to, "I just want my daddy to approve of me." In that context, she could teach her subconscious that there was no immediate threat to her self-esteem.

Later, Monique sat down with her father and explained how his statements made her feel and that, moving forward, she would appreciate it if he kept such statements to himself.

The boundary was more for Monique than for her father. She knew he'd bring it up again, and by setting the boundary, she could call out the behavior in the moment. Her subconscious would then receive the consistent messaging that her father's opinions would not dictate her own.

Monique would *allow* her father to be who he is and *allow* herself to form her own opinion of her capacity as a mother and provider.

— NINE —

Trust

There are stories I could share with you that would blow your mind. You'd even wonder how I am alive today. My best answer is that I have some badass angels and guides. And—at pivotal points in my life, I had a deep level of trust that they, God, the Universe, had my back.

It is a little weird that this is chapter nine, and nine months ago, I lost that trust for a time.

It had been brewing for a while, and I had done all the *doing* I knew how with little to no results. I consulted a good friend of mine who is an incredible psychic medium. She was honest in letting me know this wasn't something she could clear. I had my own work to do.

Ugh. More work?

Instead, I did what I have told dozens of clients to do: I threw myself an intentional pity party.

48 hours of doing absolutely nothing, binging on ice cream, and Netflix has a way of providing us with the space to process a setback. However, the rule is that it must not exceed 48 hours. This is how unintentional habits get started.

When day three arrived, I got off the couch and returned to work, but try as I might, I could not return to all aspects of my business.

In the next session with my coach, I had an epiphany. I explained that I felt like Charlie Brown trusting Lucy to hold the football while he ran to kick it–only to have her yank it away at the last second. If you've never seen it, poor Charlie falls on his ass every single time. I had grown tired of this experience and was ready for the Universe to throw me a bone. But that is not what happened.

They say we never get dealt more than we can handle, but I was tired. No. I was exhausted.

One morning, I woke up and knew exactly what I needed to do. It was time to downscale. Doing less felt counterintuitive because I wanted to level up, but something inside me knew it was necessary.

And that's when it happened. Relief. And then joy.

In releasing myself from the *shoulds* of my business, I found freedom. It struck me that I had spent the last year revving up the worthiness hustle–and by doing that hustle, I had stopped trusting in my angels, guides, and the Universe to have my back. You see, it is very difficult to *allow* if one does not trust. The expectation that my Inner Supervillain had returned to is super-common with driven women.

The expectation was, "I have to do everything myself."

Believing I had to do it all myself meant I could trust no one else, not even my angels and guides, who had been at my side in the most challenging times. I realize it may be a bit woo to say such a thing, but I hope you're used to it by now.

I think it essential to discuss the relevance of trusting from a more spiritual perspective–as it underscores how we relate to and process every event in our lives. If we continuously act on the belief that the Universe is not trustworthy enough to deliver a bit of backup when we need it, how can we find joy and hope as we work to lead from our edge and create a legacy for those who follow?

And what of the other humans in our world? If we doubt the Universe, what must we believe about them? Do we trust our family and friends to have our backs, or do we continue to insist that we have to do everything ourselves?

Jennifer worked with me for just one day. I occasionally take on a client who wants a six-hour intensive, where we focus on removing a business block. Needless to say, this often involves a personal block. But Jennifer was game to dig in and see where we went as the day progressed.

When we began, Jennifer talked about wanting to work on why she had only made slow progress growing her business that year. She wanted to sort out what might be holding her back and said she needed to know what she should energetically shift to grow faster.

"Tell me more about your typical day," I ventured.

As Jennifer described her workday, I heard exactly what I expected. Hers was a meticulously planned day, replete with household chores, shopping, cooking, working out, and a full day of business activities with calls, follow-ups, emails, design, marketing, and product positioning.

"Do you have an assistant?"

"Oh, definitely not," Jennifer replied, rolling her eyes, "I live by something my dad always said. 'Never hire anyone to do what you can do yourself.'"

"And do you live alone?"

"No."

"Does your partner share in the household duties?"

Jennifer made a yucky face and said, "Not really. I find it's just easier to just do it myself."

"Jennifer, may I ask, is there anyone who can meet your expectations?"

I knew it was a risk. But we only had a day here. I needed to get right to it. The look on her face was initially shock, then a bit of defensive anger.

"Of course," she replied with a huff.

"Can you name them?"

"Well," Jennifer looked up to the ceiling, seeking names. It was clear it was a struggle. And then she began to laugh. "I guess I can't," she said, still laughing.

I let it sit a minute or so. I could see Jennifer was processing, occasionally nodding, and having insight.

Then I asked, "Why don't you tell me when things in your business felt smoother–less blocked?"

Jennifer began describing this terrific period where any idea she had seemed to quickly come together and become a developed product.

"What did that energy feel like in your body?"

She described a "loose, open energy" full of "curiosity and playfulness." Her whole face lit up. I asked, "And did you plan for that energy to arrive?"

"No, of course not, I…" the words fell away. Jennifer realized that she had changed the way she worked along the way.

She had never expected her business to succeed. Jennifer admitted it was silly not to plan to do well, but for her, this business began as something she wanted to do for fun. And then it took off.

Feeling inadequately prepared, she had set about making a business plan and took the necessary steps to ensure further growth. Jennifer recalled feeling like such a fool to launch a business with so little preparation or effort. She hustled together a structure and grew her little company to high five-figure months. Now, however, the company's growth had leveled.

"What would it look like to return to an open energy where you were more curious and playful?"

"It would be a complete reversal." Jennifer looked pensive and a little deflated.

I let it sit a minute and finally asked, "And what would that look like?"

"I have no idea."

Again, I let it sit.

After a few minutes, Jennifer said she had just realized that whenever she dared not to have a plan, she felt incredibly guilty.

I asked if she could remember any other time in her life when she did not have a plan.

She could not. This realization clearly blew her away. Aside from the initial creation of her business, she could not recall when she did not have a plan or try to accomplish something.

As I watched Jennifer, I saw her reach back to her shoulder blades and sort of knuckle herself a mini-massage.

I leaned forward. "You know, you don't *need* to carry everyone's pain," I said.

Jennifer immediately started to cry.

I waited.

She explained that as a kid, she'd carried everyone else's work and emotional burdens and learned others could not be trusted. She had developed the habit of doing it all herself. The more work she did, the more she was praised for her strength, self-reliance, and work ethic.

As we moved forward, Jennifer realized that this lack of trust had infiltrated her entire life and created the expectation, "I have to do everything myself." This expectation was now manifesting as tension in her relationships and holding her back in her business.

Trust. A simple five-letter word.

I know it's hard. I continue to struggle with it myself. When we experience Outcome Disillusion as adults, it can trigger those trauma stories hiding in the cave with our villains.

Earning praise as a child for coping with these traumatic events only reinforces the messages and perpetuates any expectations developed along the way.

We learn to tie our worth and worthiness to what we produce and accomplish independently. We put false praise, success, or money on an altar and collect it as evidence we are worthy of love and admiration. Our worth becomes defined outside because we are not taught we are innately worthy just for 'being.'

My beautiful friend. Thank you for reading this far. You–are worthy just for being. I promise.

— TEN —

Habits

Believe it or not, driven women struggle more than men to become comfortable with the habits of allowing and letting go. Stress management techniques that involve breathing, meditation, and mindfulness are those my clients often scoff at the most.

Most claim it is because they just can't slow their minds down enough to become still. Others argue it makes them feel far too helpless and out of control. I've argued my case for meditation; there is just no one thing you can do that packs as much punch for your investment of time. Getting comfy with stillness takes practice, even if it's just five minutes at a time. I hope you will give it a try.

A couple of short chapters that follow this one will cover the daily essentials I highly recommend building into a weekly schedule; however, before I get into the meat of this chapter, I want to remind you that catching your Inner Supervillain in the act of talking shit, making overgeneralizations, or catastrophizing, is probably the most urgent habit you can form. Seeing through the PME Cycle can lead to vast awareness and stress reduction.

Let's play.

Driven women wear a lot of hats. The issue with pleasing, performing, and perfecting habits is that they enable us to wear hats without even considering what is involved. Next thing we know, we're juggling our hats as though we star in a Cirque du Soliel show in Vegas.

What I would like us to play with now is defining our hats as *we* want them to be.

Take 15 minutes and think about just these four hats for now. What are the duties each hat entails for *your life*? What do you want them to be?

I'm leaving some room for you to scribble here in the book if you'd like, but I recommend grabbing your journal and digging in.

Begin with the duties of the hat. Then, here comes the fun: Which tasks can you entrust to someone else?

When you entrust these tasks to others, let's remove the whole 'sorry to ask but' part of the request.

Let's practice with one hat:

What is the task?

Who will you ask?

How will you ask?

Fantastic! Well done! Let's keep playing.

What are the values you cherish most? Easy, right? It's okay to laugh here. None of us write down our values. But how about circling them?

Choose up to 15.

Acceptance	Dependability
Accomplishment	Design
Achievement	Discovery
Advancement	Diversity
Adventure	Environmental
Affection	Awareness
Altruism	Economic Security

Arts	Education
Awareness	Effectiveness
Beauty	Efficiency
Bravery	Elegance
Calm	Empathy
Carefulness	Entertainment
Challenge	Enlightenment
Change	Equality
Community	Ethics
Compassion	Excellence
Competence	Excitement
Connectedness	Experience
Contentment	Expertise
Cooperation	Exhilaration
Collaboration	Fairness
Country	Faith
Creativity	Fame
Decisiveness	Family
Democracy	Freedom
Friendship	Passion
Fun	Peace
Grace	Personal Development
Growth	Personal Expression
Harmony	Planning
Health	Play
Helping Others	Power
Honesty	Privacy
Humor	Quality
Imagination	Recognition
Improvement	Relationships
Independence	Reputation
Influencing Others	Resourcefulness
Inner Harmony	Responsibility

Inspiration	Risk Safety Security
Integrity	Self-Respect
Intellect	Sensibility
Involvement	Serenity
Knowledge	Skillfulness
Leadership	Service
Learning	Sophistication
Loyalty	Speculation
Making a Difference	Spirituality
Mastery	Spontaneity
Meaningful Work	Stability
Ministering	Status
Money	Strength
Morality	Success
Mystery	Tenderness
Nature	Variety
Openness	Wealth
Originality	Winning
Order	Wisdom

Okay. How did that feel? Was it difficult to choose, or was it a challenge to find 15?

I always find it harder to narrow it down to just 15 values. I want them all! So here is the real fun:

Write down just five:

_____

_____

_____

_____

_____

The cool thing is that you can change them at any time, but let's say these are your values for now.

Can you put them in order of importance to you?

1.

2.

3.

4.

5.

Congratulations! You have five values that you can now keep in front of you when creating your to-do lists. Wait. What?

Yep. Put these on a card or sticky note and play for a week. Each time you make a to-do list, weigh the entry against these values. Does it qualify? What happens if you don't complete this item today? Does it reflect your values?

Let's talk about problems. In The Crown on Netflix, British Prime Minister Winston Churchill (Played by John Lithgow) says to Queen Elizabeth II, "If there is one thing I've learned in 52 years of public service, it is that there is no problem so complex, nor crisis so grave that it cannot be satisfactorily resolved within twenty minutes."

After seeing this years ago, I gave that line some deep thought, and Churchill had a point.

What problem is so grave or complex that we should be stressing about it for days on end? Let's play with this idea by meeting our problems with a brainstorming session. Oh, and–being practical is *not* allowed.

The next time you have a problem… Okay. When that problem comes up today, set a timer, grab a marker, and get on the whiteboard. Or, a pen and paper. Or, if you really want to play, jump into Miro.com and do a brainstorming sticky note board.

Go nuts with it. Jot down every possible solution in ten minutes, no matter how 'unrealistic' it may be. Then, set your timer again for ten minutes and group your solution ideas into the following categories: Toss, Maybe, and This Could Work. Finally, decide. Of course, the decision may be to do more sleuthing for data or information, which is okay.

Congratulations! Just imagine all the stress you'll save by solving every problem in 20 minutes or less! Are you laughing with me yet? Seriously, though, give this a try and see if it doesn't prevent a few sleepless nights.

Earlier, I mentioned role-playing or writing out the dialogue with characters in our lives where we want to assert our boundaries, remember?

This is what psychologists call Stress Inoculation Training, which involves teaching coping skills to manage stress and anxiety. Training in activities such as role-playing and guided self-dialogue have shown to be an effective means for reducing performance anxiety, reducing state anxiety, and enhancing performance under stress.

The idea behind this training is that by introducing ourselves to a 'tiny dose' of the stressful situation, we effectively innoculate ourselves against the stress or anxiety of the event.

In my practice, I find that my clients benefit from rehearsing the skills around additional stressful situations, such as delegation, asking for support, or deadline negotiation.

Challenging requested deadlines is very stressful for most women. So accustomed to trying to be accommodating, the deadline in question is often treated as fixed. It doesn't even occur to us that we can both challenge and negotiate the deadline.

One way to begin negotiating a deadline is to test if it is real to begin with. Frequently, a deadline is arbitrary and meant to create false urgency. A little skepticism doesn't hurt. Jot down what questions you might ask to determine if the deadline is absolute. For example, what is the urgency and importance? What are the potential consequences of missing this deadline? Is an extension possible?

Write down three to five lines of dialogue that feel and sound like you.

Role-playing with a trusted friend, colleague, or coach can make all the difference. The important thing is to choose someone you can trust who knows why this exercise is important for you.

Play with your dialogue in different scenarios and characters, developing your responses along the way until they feel comfortable and realistic. Role-play what you would say if there were some resistance as well. Practice taking measured breaths and allowing for awkward silences.

Ensure that as you practice, you challenge yourself around the tendency to apologize. Repeat this process for delegation and asking for support, writing little scripts for practice. These exercises will help to develop a 'comfort zone' around these stressful situations and build confidence.

There is another useful habit that I mentioned earlier, and that is droning. Pulling away and observing can be crucial to maintaining or regaining a sense of calm in a trigger moment.

You'll recognize these moments more often as you work with your Inner Supervillain. At that time, ask her to stop and be still. Remember my story where I had to grip the kitchen island? Don't be afraid to close your eyes and hang on to something.

Next, imagine yourself releasing a drone from the top of your head. Guide it up and over where you are standing or sitting. What do you see? What is the situation, and what is your body doing? Try saying the phrase, "Hmm, isn't that interesting." Example: I am standing in my kitchen where I have just been opening and closing drawers with no purpose. Hmm, isn't that interesting?

Add a dash of curiosity with questions like, "I wonder why I am doing that?"

If answers float to the surface, simply repeat, "Hmm, isn't that interesting?"

The idea here is to be entirely in the moment, as a curious observer rather than a stressed-out, triggered mess. No big epiphany is required, and we are not pressured to do or create anything. It is merely an exercise in presence.

If you'd like to further explore, you can ask your body where any feelings coming to the surface may be hanging out. Remember to be curious and present. If an answer doesn't come, that is okay. If time and space permit, a little journaling afterward can be fruitful.

Back in the day, one of my favorite office supply items was that little bottle of Wite-Out. If I made an error written in permanent pen, I could easily fix it.

Now, I use the term White-Out to represent an in-the-moment correction technique with my Inner Supervillain. If I hear self-talk that does not serve me, I always have the option to tell her so and make that appointment for Sunday at 3pm. However, sometimes what is said does need immediate correction, and that's when I get out my mental White-Out.

"I'm so stupid!"

"Wait," I say, "Let's correct that." I imagine my little bottle and write the correction. "I am not only smart, but I am a genius!"

Let's summarize:

- Define your hats for how *you* want to live your life. Delegate as needed.

- Clarify your values and keep them *visible* where you make your to-do lists.

- Churchill's problem-solving. Brainstorm a problem for 20 minutes and pick a solution.

- Stress Inoculation Training, Dialogue, and roleplay stressful situations ahead of time.

- Droning. Rise above the moment, observe, and say, "Isn't that interesting?"

- White-Out. Catch your Inner Supervillain and make an instant correction.

Discussed earlier:

- Appointment setting to meet with your Inner Supervillain at a future date. Stop the mental hamster wheel, but honor the feelings.

- Keep the appointment with your Inner Supervillain, give her the space to vent, and then reign her in. Remind her you've got this.

- Body Check. Great for building trust with those villains hiding in the cave.

- PME Challenge. Take five to write down the expectation(s) and question for clarity.

— ELEVEN —

The Hour of Power

There was this time I was doubting myself and whether or not I should even be a coach. I had been speaking to my daughter about it when she exclaimed, "Mom, are you kidding? You can't even help yourself! You were born to be a coach! You coach people in line at Disneyland!"

Point taken. One of the habit practices I hand out like candy in places like the Space Mountain line at Disneyland is the Hour of Power.

Aside from thinking of my subconscious as my Inner Supervillain whom I needed to build a relationship with, the Hour of Power is probably the most impactful change I have made in my life.

It came about when I was trying to figure out how I would ever do all of the self-care activities I knew would make a big change in my life.

I kept wondering how on earth I would ever find an extra hour to meditate–and more importantly, how I would ever learn how to meditate for an hour–which seemed like an impossible amount of time to still my mind. But it was necessary.

I had just finished reading Dr. Joe Dispenza's incredible book, You Are the Placebo: Making Your Mind Matter. This book began what would later become mountains of evidence that meditation can actually heal. After all, he had done it.

I had just survived a shit storm of troubles. I was finally doing the deep inner work. My focus, for the first time… ever really, was entirely on myself.

I kept writing down these crazy schedules, where I slept for five or six hours, worked out, meditated, made my commute to work where I was a director, and stayed until seven to support my team and save a little traffic.

Then, it was errands, cooking, eating, and chores. I'd do some situps and weights, then go to bed and do some reading or journaling.

I actually pulled it off–for a while. The exhaustion and burnout caught up with me, though.

Have you ever looked back at a time in your life and asked yourself how on earth you did it? This was one of those times for me.

One day, it just came to me. Why not try to do more in less time? I realized I could shave two hours off my day and still maintain self-care.

That is when I started my Hour of Power. First thing in the morning, before anything else:

    20 minutes of workout

    20 minutes of guided meditation using an app

    20 minutes of journaling with my coffee

I started with just ten minutes of working out. Within two weeks, I was up to 20 minutes.

I then added the meditation right in. The app had several 20-minute meditations to choose from, so I kept trying them until I found one I really wanted to stick with.

Journaling over coffee became the reward. Then, I could hit the shower feeling an entirely new level of peace mixed with energy.

As time went on, this practice changed my life.

Did I just catch you rolling your eyes? Is it possible a list of reasons why this would be particularly difficult for you is being written in your head at this very moment? If not, congratulations! You are a unicorn!

However, if you are making that list, you aren't alone. Almost everyone I share the Hour of Power with starts telling me why they can't possibly do it. But that is the PME Cycle hard at work.

Perception: Danger! Danger! Pain ahead!

Meaning-making: The last time we tried to work out in the mornings, it was a disaster, remember? Besides, 20 minutes isn't really enough to make a difference. And we don't have equipment! This just doesn't work for us. No, thank you.

Expectation: I have to be a wonder woman at managing my life to fit an hour of self-care into my day.

Wait. Did you catch that?

Why didn't I write that I'm too busy to fit an hour of self-care into my day? That's the truth, isn't it?

Let me ask you–is it? Does your subconscious really believe that you are too busy? Or is it full of self-defeating beliefs about how, if you were good enough, only then would it be possible?

That is the thing with the PME Cycle. Sometimes, we really need to read between the lines of the meaning-making language to see the actual expectation behind it. It helps to write it as an expectation, which usually starts with 'I have to.'

Whenever there's cognitive dissonance–in this case, listing off a bunch of reasons we can't do a thing we know we really can do, there is likely a PME Cycle behind it. That is your Inner Supervillain working hard to change your belief to "I don't have the time."

If she is successful, change and pain don't have to happen, and you can continue as before.

Therefore, it is necessary to watch for The PME Cycle so the expectation can come to the surface where it can be challenged.

Expectation: I have to be a wonder woman at managing my life to fit an hour of self-care into my day.

Question: Is that true?

Answer: Of course it's true! Let's look at the examples we have lined up for why we are too busy. *Starts to rattle off the calendar.*

And we just go with that? How about we delve deeper into this story:

Question: Do we absolutely *have to* do all that stuff?

Answer: Well, no.

Question: Then why are we doing it?

Answer: Because it makes us feel important, valuable, praised, successful, capable, etc.

Now that we have that out of the way, how about looking at your schedule to see if you can get that Hour of Power in?

What else can you let go of?

Do you *really* have to do *everything* currently on your list? Could some things be pared down or removed altogether?

What would the benefits be of working out 20 minutes each morning, five days per week, if you aren't already?

What are the potential benefits of incorporating a daily meditation practice?

What would it feel like to invest 20 minutes a day with a pen and a journal?

Give it some thought. I hope you decide to try it.

– TWELVE –

Thriving 90

Over the course of seven years, I have designed six workbooks and four planners. I initially made a workbook for myself because I knew I wanted to track my Hour of Power in three parts and work with my Inner Supervillain every week.

As I wrote this first workbook, other concepts emerged that created accountability for my deep inner work.

Soon, family and friends wanted a copy, and as I outgrew each edition, I'd share these workbooks and planners with family, friends, and then clients. Some of us just like to have a way to document this work. However, I have also had clients who would have tossed the workbook or planner in the trash, which is okay, too. Some people get the insight and run with it. Others need homework and steady reflection to see the insight through to fruition.

I really wanted to share stories in this book that provide some insight. However, I also wanted to include actionable techniques and strategies.

One such strategy is the habit of Thriving 90.

In the last planner I made for myself, I was looking to simplify what had previously been a series of workbooks with detailed goal planning and a ton of pages dedicated toward the deep inner work. Now, I do most of that work in my morning journaling.

I found a terrific company called Plum Paper, where I could jump online and design the most important aspects of a nice-looking planner, but they handle the overall design.

I was able to add "Lead From Your Edge" to the front and then choose the 'daily' style of planner. The cool part is being able to label the various sections on the pages. One such area at the top had three highlighted spaces. I customized and labeled it "Thriving 90" without yet knowing why. This happens to me occasionally, where I receive what some call a 'download.

It has occurred so many times now that I just roll with it. I knew this would be my new habit, and in a sudden flash, I realized why.

After spending over a year talking to incredible entrepreneurs about the danger of burning out, I ended up experiencing burnout myself. Stepping back was the wisest decision I've made in my business. It allowed me to reprioritize and spend time on the projects I was truly passionate about.

We tell ourselves and each other that if we are passionate about the work, it isn't work at all. And while it is true that there is much less drudgery involved, passion doesn't prevent burnout.

It is quite possible to pile iron upon iron into the fire of passion. Commitment without question to projects we love is why our values are so vital when considering our to-do lists. There needs to be a vocabulary to help us sort the hell-yes projects from the rest.

Along with keeping dialed-in to our values is the importance of consistent self-care.

Beyond the bubble bath or occasional massage, caring for ourselves is something we should each be doing every single day. And while dismissing self-care as impossible is common among driven women, ignoring it can result in extreme burnout.

I started working with Brenda after she came to Vegas for vacation. She asked me to come by the hotel and have a chat over lunch. Having known her personally for a time, I was surprised when she suggested she needed a coach. I usually avoid working with friends or relatives, but I made an exception for her because she seemed desperate.

Brenda was burned out. She had been caring for everyone but herself. There were the girls and then her boyfriend, who needed help with his estate paperwork. Along with his various holdings and accounts, there was a complicated medical situation with his niece. Brenda didn't hesitate to step in and ensure the niece was well cared for, going so far as to travel to another state to get the niece settled into a new home.

What Brenda described was dedicated loyalty well beyond what anyone would expect. However, as she explained her situation, I noted the repeated negative talk about her failure to manage her health. She was blind to the reasons behind her burnout.

"Has Alex considered hiring an assistant?"

"Oh no, I would never let him do that," Brenda protested, "That would be such a waste of money."

She went on to tell me about Alex's son, who lived with them, and finally, her own health issues.

Brenda explained that on that very morning, they had to call a doctor to the hotel because she couldn't breathe. The doctor had suggested she consider returning directly home for treatment. She wouldn't hear of it, though, because family and friends were coming from various locations to spend the day in a rented cabana. Brenda wanted to ensure they had a terrific time and said they were looking forward to using the lazy river. She took the opportunity to invite me to stay and have a glass of wine as well. That was the moment I agreed to work with her.

In our early sessions, Brenda would apologize almost every week for not being a good client. Her expectations of herself were very high, and her Inner Supervillain was focused on the negative.

During the next eight weeks, Brenda began to develop a loving friendship with her subconscious and could see how over-extended she was.

Decades of pleasing, performing, and perfecting habits don't just disappear with our awareness, though. It was many more weeks until Brenda could say what she wanted for herself without apology, and many more before she could admit it was time to set some boundaries around the relationships in her life.

Predictably, there were many setbacks along the way, and Brenda's health became a challenge several times. And then something shifted.

About five months into our sessions, it became clear that Brenda had recognized she deserved to be happy and that she, not her Inner Supervillain, would be making choices to further that cause.

A trip was planned where Brenda would visit friends, and she took the opportunity to sit Alex down and set some boundaries. While Brenda was away, he would have to manage his own affairs.

The day that I knew the significant shift had happened was when Brenda told me she had started to spend mornings outside with her coffee alone.

Stillness is a massive hurdle for the driven woman. To make an actual habit of it is Herculean.

In that stillness, Brenda could journal for the first time in many years. This led to some incredible breakthroughs. In our sessions, I could really see the difference from the overwrought Brenda, who had invited me to lunch. The shift was remarkable.

In stillness, our presence is born.

As women accustomed to *doing* our way through problems, it can feel counterproductive to choose stillness. In fact, it is pretty common to use being busy in order to avoid feelings that may come up in stillness. Through intentional stillness, we can practice quiet observation and acceptance, elect to disown the hysterical woman narrative, and develop a relationship with our subconscious.

There is another benefit to stillness. I tease my clients that it allows lighting to strike.

A few months ago, I was frustrated trying to write something about why coaching is so powerful. I wanted an easy-to-send description, but nothing was working. I kept *trying* but made no progress.

To make matters worse, my schedule that week was packed. I had an engagement in California, clients, and plans with my daughter. I was a bit overextended. Yeah, I know–I'm supposed to be this fantastic coach who doesn't make these errors in judgment, right?

Wrong.

Fortunately, that Wednesday, I had planned to take the car in for an oil change and mileage check-up. That meant 2-3 hours sitting in the dealership waiting room with all the coffee I could drink. I grabbed that new planner of mine and some colored pens.

Filling out my planner took all of 20 minutes. I had already made a deal with myself that I would not spend this time on my friggin' phone.

I sat.

I fought it for a moment.

Then, I allowed myself to... breathe.

Whammo!

Lightning struck! I remembered my analogy about how coaching is like climbing a mountain, and this whole visual popped into my head. I grabbed my planner and used old daily pages to draw a series of unartistic stick-woman scenes.

And then I wrote this:

Let me tell you a story....

A Leader is on her path. She's got it all going on, but life has its challenges, right?

One day, this leader slips and falls into this cavernous hole. Try as she might, she sees no way out.

Along comes an expert, schooled in the 1001 ways to get yourself out of the hole. The expert tosses her book and a flashlight down and merrily walks on.

The Leader reads the book. There's great stuff inside! The book provides valuable insight.

However, the Leader soon realizes that the tools she needs to get out of this hole are more than what is provided in the book. She feels frustrated. How will she ever get out of this hole?

Next comes a speaker, full of great advice and a vision for the Leader's future. She even throws down paper and pen so she can take notes as she gives her motivational talk.

The Leader is inspired and takes copious notes. She visualizes her future and knows she can succeed.

However… the Leader looks around and realizes she's still in this damn hole. After a while, she begins to believe there's just no getting out. After all, she's read the expert's book and even has a ton of notes and a vision of her future from the motivational speaker! In fact, as she looks around again, she could swear she's even deeper in this hole. The Leader begins to feel hopeless.

Suddenly, she looks up and sees a friendly face. This gal doesn't look like an expert. In fact, she has bruises and dirt on her face. She does look prepared for climbing, though. "Hi! I'm a coach! You look like you could use some help!" The Leader feels some hope. Maybe she'll pull her out of this damn hole.

Instead, though, the coach climbs down into the hole.

"What are you doing?" she shouts up at the coach.

"Meeting you where you are!" the coach replies with a smile, wiping dirt from her face with the back of her hand. The Leader doesn't see how this is going to help, but she must confess–it feels good not to be alone down in this hole.

The Leader and the coach share some time together in the hole. After a couple of powerful conversations, the coach shares some tools with the Leader and encourages her to make her first attempts to get out of the hole.

The Leader begins to climb, and even though she doesn't like to show fear, she confesses that she might not be ready for this level.

"This is harder than I expected!" the Leader says.

The coach replies, "I know. This is a different area of expertise, and there are new things to learn. But now you have the tools. You've got this!"

The Leader makes her way higher but again doubts herself, and she falls.

"Ugh! I hate this!" shouts the Leader. "I don't like feeling like a failure! This is what I was afraid of!"

The coach smiles and reaches out a hand. "I know it hurts. But look at what you've learned here. And let's talk about your progress. You know that it takes failures to make progress. It's just that no one else expects you to fail, right? And you don't want to let them down."

The Leader and coach have a few more powerful conversations about being a driven woman and other people's expectations.

The leader gets even better at using her tools. She climbs again. The coach encourages, listens, and continues to challenge her as she climbs. When she makes it to the top, she realizes a few things:

First, that the coach had never left her alone in the hole. She was always with her.

Second, that while this was true, she had gotten herself out of the hole without so much as a boost. All she ever needed was the tools and a good coach who had the expertise to get out of the hole–but also understood the journey because she had been there herself.

Finally, as she dusted herself off, she knew that after this, there was no dream too big. She could do anything. But it sure was nice to know she didn't have to dream alone.

Not bad, right? That was my first draft, as written on planner pages, because I allowed myself a bit of stillness instead of grabbing for my phone to distract myself. It isn't perfect. But I will share with you that when I read it to my own coach later that day, it made me cry. I love what coaching can do. I love my coach, and I am so grateful to be able to work with her month after month.

I also love being a coach. I love that when I meet another driven woman who needs out of the hole, I get to say, "Hi! It looks like you could use a little help!"

I love learning about her–what drives her, what fires her up, and most of all, watching her use the tools and techniques in new ways to make magic happen. I love that I get to be in the room.

And that brings me to the more straightforward explanation that Thriving 90 is what I practiced that day. Thriving 90 is stillness, but not inactivity.

There are only a few guidelines:

- It can be in increments of at least 30 minutes throughout the day.
- Aim for three, but be proud of one.
- The phone is elsewhere.
- Coloring, journaling, writing without a clear purpose, and just looking at the trees, flowers, and chirping birds are all highly encouraged.

Of course, you can make your own guidelines.

I definitely do not get all 90 minutes every day. I am getting better at it, and you will, too.

Maybe lightning will strike.

— THIRTEEN —

Unmasking Emotional Triggers

Imagine yourself as Super-You. You've embarked on a transformative inner growth journey and walk with newfound awareness and confidence.

You've honed the art of setting and maintaining boundaries, integrating insightful practices into your daily routine. Life has been on an upswing, and you're basking in the glory of your evolved self.

And then, it happens–a trigger. It could be a word, a sight, a scent, a touch, or a taste, but suddenly, you find yourself plummeting, unable to regain your footing.

In this bewildering moment, it feels as though your Inner Supervillain jumped on your back and is now orchestrating a playback of old, haunting VHS tapes while munching on chips. At this moment, she doesn't feel like your ally.

Both as a coach and client, I can relate.

As a coach, I have seen it coming–the inevitable moment when my client stumbles, triggered by circumstances, whether for a fleeting moment or an enduring stretch.

As a client, I know it will happen. Yet, it often sneaks up on me, leaving me to lament with my coach, "Why is this happening? I thought I learned this shit already!"

Here is what we must acknowledge:

First, life is cyclical. What goes around tends to come around again. Sure, there might be nuances to explore, but sometimes, it's the same old challenges wearing different disguises. Lessons must be learned or revisited–it's an inescapable part of the journey.

Second, our Inner Supervillain is our subconscious in action. She's our autopilot, the sum of our past experiences and conditioning. Yes, she can be reprogrammed, but it's a process that demands time and dedication.

The inconvenient truth is that certain aspects of our autopilot may forever remain etched during our formative years or by traumatic events.

Because we are meant to repeat some lessons, practicing self-compassion becomes crucial. Within this triggering experience lies an opportunity for growth, and by allowing this emotional tide to flow through us, rather than resisting or evading it, we can expedite our evolution.

Or, to extend the analogy, if we attempt to forcefully remove our Inner Supervillain, our subconscious will only tighten its grip, convinced it's safeguarding us.

Let's be candid–the experience of being triggered, well, it sucks. Triggers can resurrect ancient memories and replay outdated scripts, often accompanied by intense emotions and visceral sensations. They strike so swiftly at times that we're caught in a whirlwind, reacting before we can even think.

Regulating and responding to our emotions plays a pivotal role in our mental health. Dr. James Gross, in 1998, described emotion regulation as the processes through which individuals control which emotions they experience, when they experience them, and how they express those emotions. This concept becomes particularly intriguing when we delve into the realm of impulsive and compulsive behaviors.

When the trigger moment occurs, we experience an overwhelming emotion. It may be anxiety, anger, shame, or even an intense burst of positive feelings. How are we regulating these emotions?

According to the research by Gross and other scholars, virtually any behavior that is under our voluntary control and influences our mood can also be used as a tool for regulating our emotions.

To put it more simply, Impulsive-compulsive (or I-C) behaviors like problem eating, gambling, shopping, and others can be our way of coping with our unpleasant emotions or trauma.

Pent-up or hidden emotions like anger or shame can drive us to seek release or escape using misguided regulation techniques such as smoking, alcohol consumption, and more.

Positive effects can also be a trigger. Some of us may resort to I-C behaviors not to reduce distress but to prolong the pleasurable feelings we are experiencing. For example, someone might engage in excessive shopping or substance use to maintain a state of euphoria.

When we are triggered by intense emotions such as shame or anger, our subconscious mind often resorts to impulsive or compulsive behaviors as a protective mechanism. These behaviors shield against the overwhelming pain of the original traumatic event or emotional trigger. Our Inner Supervillain will instinctively choose the path of least resistance, seeking immediate relief from the emotional turmoil.

In this intricate dance of emotions and behaviors, it is the subconscious force that drives us towards impulsive actions to cover or avoid the pain of the originating traumatic event.

While impulsive behaviors offer a quick fix, seeming to soothe the emotional turmoil, they also leave a trail of long-term consequences.

Conversely, compulsivity is a repetitive, ritualistic response to the emotional trigger, which offers us the illusion of control but ultimately exacerbates the underlying emotional pain.

In both cases, impulsive and compulsive behaviors serve as distractions, a way to numb the pain or divert attention from the root cause of our emotional distress.

Understanding the intricate relationship between emotional triggers, impulsivity, compulsivity, and our inner supervillain sheds light on the complex nature of human behavior. Emotions are powerful forces that can drive us to engage in behaviors we might not fully comprehend.

The deep inner work I keep going on about really is a critical journey toward greater self-awareness and, ultimately, a more balanced and fulfilling life.

That established–what do we do in that moment of trigger to regain our balance and, hopefully, get our Inner Supervillain off our back?

We have examined at least ten habits, but this one deserves particular attention. 8-4-8 rhythmic breathing is my go-to for trigger moments.

This is not Dr. Andrew Weil's 4-7-8 method.

Instead, this is a long, slow diaphragmatic belly intake breath of eight seconds, followed by a hold of four seconds, then a long, intentional release breath of eight seconds.

I like to sit up cross-legged, but I also do this breathing in the car, shower, sitting on the couch ready to cry–you name it.

First, the intake breath: Breathe in through your nose slowly enough to count to eight, allowing your belly to fill. If you get to six or seven and feel like you have run out of breath, you can purse your lips and suck in some extra air as if through a straw until you reach eight.

Then, hold it for four seconds.

The release breath: Purse your lips as if to whistle and exhale slowly from your mouth, counting to eight. Press your belly button toward your spine.

Depending on the magnitude of the trigger, I may need just a minute or two of this breathing or several.

Now is the time for a few gentle questions:

- Do I know what this trigger is about?

- Can I name the emotion?

- Where in the body is this emotion?

- Is it essential to unpack right now?

Don't fuss over the order of the questions. Sometimes, the body's reaction will feel so strong it claims your attention.

Remember that our Inner Supervillain will look for the path of least resistance. She may have alerted your amygdala to fire up the hypothalamus and issued the order, "Send in the stress hormones!"

When considering your body, you may notice the fight/flight symptoms of a racing heart, quickened breath, and tense muscles. But what else do you notice?

Naming the emotion can be handy, particularly when it doesn't match the scenario.

For me, asking if I know what the trigger is about is extremely helpful because, almost always, it is about something other than what is in front of me.

Considering if it really needs to be unpacked right, this moment is a terrific way of talking ourselves down and regulating more healthily.

Trigger moments can create turmoil. But within this turmoil lies a silver lining—a chance for deeper understanding and personal growth. With practice, you can learn to embrace the discomfort as part of your journey, for it's in these moments that you have the opportunity to transform and evolve into an even more resilient and self-aware version of Super-You.

— FOURTEEN —

Conclusion

All of my life, I have wanted to help others. I remember being just six or seven years old, thinking I'd like to be a teacher and writer, just like Laura Ingalls Wilder.

I also recall suffering in silence as a former abuse victim at twelve or thirteen. It seemed at the time that no one understood me and that no one ever would. But in the dark, I looked up at the ceiling and said aloud, "Someday, I'm going to write a book for others like me, and it will help them."

Many years later, as a teacher, I stood before my students and told them they could be anything. I said it year after year with such conviction and passion some of those kids believed me.

Later, I dedicated myself to coaching and training teachers and leaders, knowing they would, in turn, impact hundreds and thousands of other people.

In these last six years, it has been my honor to run workshops for and speak to hundreds of women from all over the globe–But it is through my work as a coach to individual driven women that I really feel my soul shine–until now.

Writing this book has been soul-guided for sure. While it unfortunately doesn't ensure that it will be widely read, or even that it's good, I can honestly say that I was meant to write it.

Somewhere, my Soul-Ship Pirate Captain is smiling as she checks off this book from her list.

Oh–you know I love a good analogy, right? I like to think of my highest self as my Soul-Ship Pirate Captain, sailing the waves of the Universe, all brilliant and badass. Based on a book I read by Gary Zukov, I've always imagined many me's, living many different lives in many other spaces. But my Soul-Ship Pirate Captain guides us all.

It's terrific imagery, and I keep an illustrated lady pirate in my office to re-mind me that there is a higher me, inspiring me to live unapologetically, reach for more without guilt, and seek adventure.

By now, if you have gotten this far, you have already had moments of insight and inspiration that will help you work to ditch the worthiness hustle.

The dilemma of driven women should not be how to have it all by doing it all–pushing through and enduring record levels of stress, anxiety, and disease. Instead, we should seize the choice as to how we *prefer* to live our lives to get *most* of what we really want while maintaining high-quality, impactful, stress-resistant lives.

In my office, I started a sticky note door. Initially, it began with the things I wanted to talk about or coach on. Over the last three years, it has be-come the four pillars of my work with leaders navigating Driven Woman Syndrome.

This book is pillar one: Awareness. It is not meant to stand on its own, nor should it be considered a complete guide on ditching your worthiness hustle. That said, I am proud to have shared pillar one with you, and now, you have some tools to be selective and strategic about when, why, and on whom you spend your valuable time and personal resources. You know that pleasing, performing, and perfecting your way through life won't work in the long run.

Thank you for reading this book. What happens next is up to you.

ACKNOWLEDGEMENTS

Mom– Thank you for keeping me, choosing the hard way, showing me the power of art, and teaching me many, many things. I love you.

Pop– Thank you for encouraging me to love the written word, inspiring in me such a love of music, and daring to chase your dreams.

Dad– Thank you for reconnecting with me and giving me a whole new family on the other side of the world.

Nick– Buddy, wherever you are, know that "I'll love you forever, I'll like you for always, As long as I'm living, My baby you'll be."

Anna– You've always been my partner-in-crime. Thank you for writing that essay when you were a kid and always believing I am braver than I believe, stronger than I seem, and smarter than I think. I am so grateful for what we share.

Auntie– Your presence still keeps me afloat.

Bryan– Thank you for being at my side all those times and for being there still.

Joa– Thank you for remembering.

Grandma– You spicy, filterless, incredible woman. Thank you. And Elvis will always be in my kitchen.

Grandpa– Thank you for reminding me you are there. It means so much.

Ella– Thank you for reminding me I have so much strong woman DNA. I value it and honor you.

Trina– I have never been so grateful for a friggin' FB group! Thank you so much for your invaluable friendship and support. I can't wait for what's next!

Lisa– You never forget me, and I am so grateful for that. Thank you so much for seeing me when I did not and for being there.

My private clients– You bring me alive and remind me why I am here. I honor your journeys, path, commitment, courage, and the way you are redefining what it means to be a driven woman for generations that come after you. You are the game changers.

RESOURCES

Elite private coaching

Generally by invitation and referral only, there is often a waitlist. You are always welcome to inquire@leadfromyouredge.co

VIP

As my Elite client, there is a VIP opportunity to travel to exotic locations and immerse into your wellness, featuring exclusive experiences and excursions and building connections with an intimate selection of like-minded leaders like you.

Lead From Your Edge

Livestream on YouTube every Sunday at 3pm PST.

The Burnout Cure

A self-guided, ten-lesson program for professional women on the verge of or experiencing burnout.

Speaking and Workshops

Keynote: The Power of Unapologetic Leadership

Stop apologizing! Put the force and precision back into your leadership style by being more resilient, powerful, and intentional in how you lead as a woman.

Take Yourself Seriously:

A Crash Course in Confidence

Overcome imposter syndrome and learn what it feels like to create self-acceptance, love, and trust in yourself. Tap into your passion and intuition and make today the someday you've been waiting for.

Wild Femmepreneur has an Impact Plan:

10% of all company profits go to Thistle Farms, an incredible, thriving sanctuary for women survivors of trafficking, prostitution, and addiction.

Learn more about what they do at:

Thistlefarms.org

On A Mission

As part of our Impact Plan, I have reserved two monthly slots for intensive, private coaching. Meant to serve women who otherwise would be unable to work with a private coach, the fees are just $1,200 for four weeks and will remain unchanged for those clients.

If you know someone who you think would benefit from this tremendous opportunity, please have them reach out to us directly at:

impact@wildfemmepreneur.com

ABOUT THE AUTHOR

CHARLIE McCLAIN is a respected thought leader and private executive coach. In the world of personal development, her powerful talks and workshops focus on leadership and the intricacies of Driven Woman Syndrome. Through her weekly show, Lead From Your Edge, Charlie supports and challenges executives and leaders as they strive toward new frontiers, professionally and personally.

As a driven woman who went from being an educator and business owner, living a millionaire lifestyle–to arriving homeless in a shelter for battered women–then courageously rebuilding her life as a professional and entrepreneur, Charlie isn't quite like any other executive coach you've encountered. Through a wide array of techniques and practices, she calls the Soul Quotient™, Charlie helps the women she works with become unshakable in the face of the complexities of modern-day living and leading.

With two decades of experience and a Master's in Education, she began a series of research projects on the subconscious, beliefs, and meditation. As Charlie pursued her second Master's degree in Psychology, she focused her research on Driven Woman Syndrome. This work, her inspirational experiences, and her use of digestible analogies are the bedrock of Charlie's programs, talks, and workshops.

Charlie is an International speaker, bestselling contributing author, Executive Contributor for Brainz Magazine, and Crea Global Award recipient, featured in USA Today, Fox, NBC, and more.

She is a native of California, but in 2020, she moved to Las Vegas, Nevada.

www.ingramcontent.com/pod-product-compliance
Lightning Source LLC
Chambersburg PA
CBHW060436090426
42733CB00011B/2289